MUMBAI
to STOCKHOLM
via NEW YORK

MUMBAI
to STOCKHOLM
via NEW YORK

PEOPLE, PLACES AND POLITICS
REFLECTIONS OF A GLOBETROTTER

DAN MAYUR

To order additional copies of this book, contact:
Xlibris Corporation
1-888-795-4274
www.Xlibris.com
Orders@Xlibris.com
107163

CONTENTS

PART III
SCANDINAVIA

To
Mummiji, Neela, Anita, and Samir
for
Your love, support, and encouragement

PREFACE

If you picked this book up to read about the famous Icebar in Stockholm or to locate the best Indian restaurant in New York, you will not find it here. This is not a travelogue.

In our dynamic world, the winds of change are blowing hard today. Entrenched for decades, powerful governments in autocratic countries are toppling without military force through the power of social media. The global financial markets are in turmoil. Fortunes are being made, and life savings are being destroyed. In democratic countries like the US and India, the establishments are threatened by grassroots movements demanding change. In the globalized world, with instant communication and few barriers, what happens in one corner of the world has an immediate impact on the other.

This book is a collection of essays written over the past two years during my travels around the world in this changing environment. The essays primarily pertain to the problems and the changes happening in three parts of the world—India, the United States, and Scandinavia with particular reference to Sweden. They offer a curious traveler's ground-level view of the socioeconomic aspects of these countries.

The essays are grouped by countries in three parts of the book, but they can be read independently in any order. In reading a collection like this, there is a tendency to try to find a common theme across all essays. The discerning reader will have no difficulty in recognizing that the focus here is the life of the common man in the rapidly changing globalized world where physical, geographical, and cultural boundaries are breaking down rapidly.

This book is intended to entertain and inform a mature readership. It will appeal to general readers, students, travelers, and people with specific interest in the US, India, and Scandinavia. The essays deal with issues of current interest—election politics, economy, energy, transportation, religion, women's equality, and general aspects of daily life with specific reference to the three regions. The essays are descriptive of the current conditions but provide historical perspective and analysis where appropriate. It is expected that after reading all the essays about a country, the reader will get a general sense of the quality of life there, its prevailing situation, and future outlook.

I have chosen the three regions in this book for specific reasons. The world's future is in democracy, notwithstanding the dramatic advance of China in recent years. But democracies come in different shapes and sizes. The US represents the most successful, affluent, and oldest democracy and has been a magnet for immigrants from all over the world. Located diametrically opposite on the globe is India, the largest democracy in the world. With almost four times the population of the United States, India has a growing economy and an aspiring middle class. It is becoming a major player in the global market. The country has its own unique set of struggles, challenges, and growing pangs. In comparison, Scandinavia has a small, maturing population and its own brand of socialism with its highly successful economic model.

I have spent almost all my life in the US, India, and Scandinavia. My roots are Indian, education and experience American, and mind-set Scandinavian. I was born in India. I immigrated to the US as a graduate student at the age of twenty-one. I have resided there continuously until the past six years when I started spending the better part of every year in Sweden. America has been my home and has been wonderful to me.

The first essay I wrote for this book was about Scandinavia during my first visit there a few years ago. Before that, I knew very little about the region or Scandinavian socialism. I was mesmerized by the relative affluence and the clean, quiet, and relaxed life and the overall sense of happiness among the people there.

Leaving Scandinavia for India with its chaotic dynamism was a major eye-opener. It was also difficult returning back to America with its innovative but pervasive commercialization. After a short absence from a place, you suddenly see there what you never saw before. You are bothered by things that never bothered you before; you miss things that you never missed before.

It was evident that the sociopolitical environments in the US and India were changing dramatically, for the better in some ways, for the worse in others. It was also clear that the best and the worst of humanity coexisted in these two bastions of democracy. In the summer of 2011, all of a sudden came the news of the brutal massacre of innocent people in peace-loving Norway. That was a truly brain freezing experience for me. However, one thing was clear—people all over the world, although in different political and economic circumstances, are similar and have the same concerns, aspirations, and problems. The differences are mostly superficial.

This book presents a world seen through the eyes of an empathetic, interested observer. I have no specific agenda to promote. My effort is to present a balanced view of India, USA, and Scandinavia whose democracies are in different phases of maturity. If countries were people, India would be like a boisterous twenty-year-old, struggling, making his mistakes and learning, getting lost and eventually finding his way. The country has enormous potential based on its youth and energy. America would be a mature, well-established, and successful adult of forty-five. Scandinavia would look like an accomplished senior citizen who is leading a peaceful and affluent life near retirement age. The commentary in the essays is intended to identify the problem areas and offer constructive suggestions for betterment of the lands I love so dearly.

I am happy about my Scandinavian experience, thankful about American opportunities, and hopeful about the future of India. In a familial metaphor, India is my mother that influenced me and raised me as a child. America is the loving spouse who has enriched my life and to whom I am committed. Lastly, Sweden is a cherished dear friend.

I trust that the reader will view my critique in this light.

Dan Mayur
December 2011
Sugar Land, Texas

ACKNOWLEDGMENTS

The writing of this book was akin to a team sport, not a game of solitaire. I could not have done it without a host of wonderful people around me to challenge, supplement, and enrich my ideas. It would have been impossible without their knowledge, sense of humor, and stories to sustain me. This experience has taught me that writing a book really "takes a village."

This book is the product of my observations and experiences during my travels in various parts of the world. My views are the results of numerous informal discussions, debates, and arguments with dear friends over a cup of cappuccino, or at times pizza and beer.

I am deeply indebted to my wonderful friends Peter and Ann-Sofi Freyhult, Karl and Kristina Elfstadius, Christopher and Jeanette Carlander, Boris Bengtsson, Marina Ohrn, Knut Faber, Johan and Ingeborg Andersson, Claus Vetter, Stefan and Sandra Bengtzing for highly stimulating discussions on the current situation in the US, Europe, and Scandinavia. Peter and Ann-Sofi are walking encyclopedias, and I am sure they never have to google anything about Scandinavia. Karl has been around the globe over a hundred times and brought an insightful perspective to our debates. Marina contributed her thoughtful observations of life in the US and Sweden in her inimitable witty manner. Claus, an avid Indophile, who knows India as well as his native Germany, brought his wealth of detailed understanding to our discussions.

My classmates from the Indian Institute of Technology in Bombay read many of the essays in this book and gave me valuable comments for improvement. I am particularly thankful to Professor Kesav Nori of the Indian Institute of Information Technology, Professor Kalyan Singhal of the University of Baltimore, Vijay Kulkarni and Jitendra Bhatia for their review of my essays.

I am thankful to my friends Suchitra Vazirani, Viju Bhadkamkar, and Dr. Shivani Sethi for their suggestions and encouragement. Suchitra is among my most widely traveled and well-read friends. I found our discussions during my stay in idyllic Kaivalyadham valuable in writing my essays on India. Jyoti Prakash Saraf and Subhash Saraf took time from their busy schedules to read various essays and provided interesting Indian perspectives as did Sonali and Chetan Dhruve.

Many of my ideas about the world, and particularly the United States, were challenged, refined, and crystallized after several invigorating and enlightening discussions with my wonderful friends Doug and Michele Timmerberg and Matt Kerin. Thank you, Doug, Michele, and Matt.

I gratefully acknowledge the contributions of my family support team and cheerleaders—my siblings and their spouses, Ranjana, Dr. Nitin, Sangeeta, Kiran, Bina, Abhay, Roma, and Gopi who read every one of my essays as they were written offering helpful comments and corrections as they went along.

Reading the entire manuscript of someone's writing is very demanding of time. I cannot thank enough my friend Suresh Gurjar for taking on the review and treating it as a serious workplace assignment. He critiqued and edited the manuscript with extraordinary promptness and attention to detail. I am thankful to Avinash Pandit for his professional review and constructive comments. He is one of the best in the business.

While I have immensely benefitted from the input from these wonderful people, I alone am responsible for any shortcomings of the book.

One person who single-handedly drove this entire project is my artist-architect friend Anita Kulkarni. She compiled, organized, edited the essays, and designed the cover of the book. She has been a valuable adviser and a cheerleader from the beginning to the end. This book would not have been possible without Anita's enthusiasm and tireless efforts. My appreciation for Anita's help is beyond words.

I could not have been involved in a project like this without the understanding and support of my family. I do not have adequate words to thank my mother, Mummiji, who has always been a supporter, inspirer, and a guide throughout my life. I am thankful to my wife, Neela, for her incomparable cheer and unlimited patience. She read the book many times, possibly memorizing a number of pages. She did this without losing her cool, but every time changing a word here or a sentence there, trying to make me a better writer. My harshest critics were my children, Anita and Samir. Anita made sure that the manuscript was clean, correct, and balanced. Samir ensured that this book did not embarrass him or me. I have more than a few torn up versions of the manuscript thanks to Samir and Anita's aggressive quality control.

This one is for you Mummiji, Neela, Anita, and Samir for your unconditional love, support, and encouragement.

INDIA

The Qutub Minar, Delhi
A prominent example of Indo-Islamic architecture

ONE

EWR to BOM

Liberty International Airport in Newark is one of New York City's three major airports. The Newark to Mumbai direct flight is usually filled with people of Indian origin. They typically travel in assorted groups—families with young children, elderly grandparents, and the new crop of twenty-something IT professionals. This is a wonderful opportunity for an interested social observer to study fellow human beings. It affords an early exposure to Brand India. On an individual basis, Indians are among the friendliest, most hospitable, and generous people in the world. Frequently, this private goodness fails to translate into the public life. The corruption in India may well be a reflection of the mind-set and routine activities of the Indian people.

After a three-hour uneventful flight from Houston, I arrived in New York around 3:30 PM. My flight to India was from the Newark Liberty International Airport, one of the three major airports serving the area. It is conveniently located in New Jersey just across the Hudson River. I had several hours before my 8:30 PM flight to Mumbai, but as is my habit, I wandered around to my designated gateway ahead of time only to find that my fellow passengers had already turned Gate C-98 into a little India of sorts. Apparently, half of Edison, New Jersey, that may have the largest concentration of Gujaratis outside of Gujarat was going to fly with me. (Disclosure: I am a Gujarati). The place was replete with the sights, sounds, and smells that define Brand India, and my much anticipated trip to India had started some eighteen hours before my actual landing there.

BRAND INDIA

Wherever any Indians come together, be it in London or New York or Singapore, regardless of age, education, or income level, the group behavior is unmistakably characterized by a peculiar nodding of heads, high-pitched loud talking, and unruly kids noisily running around their unconcerned parents. No matter these same kids, a few years down the road, will respectfully start addressing all elders as uncles and aunts and will be more likely to be admitted to the Harvards and Yales than any other ethnic group. Undoubtedly, these unsupervised little brats are among the most annoying, but nobody seems to mind it except a curmudgeon like me. One thing for sure—you can take Indians out of India, but you cannot take India out of Indians no matter where they go.

Four distinct groups were clearly evident among the passengers—grandpas, grandmas, kids, and IT professionals. This last group, mostly single men, invariably toting a laptop and many of them in faded and torn jeans and sporting incongruent and utterly pointless baseball caps (NY Yankees!) must have thought that they were making the highest fashion statement of the times by dressing as their favorite Bollywood heroes do in modern India. Grandmas, typically three times the size of their emaciated spouses, are the most voluble of the group. In contrast, the grandpas are the quietest and are typically bundled up in a crumpled jacket with a long-sleeve sweater inside, a scarf around the neck, and some kind of a headgear, all of various colors and patterns. The more sophisticated ones wear a tie but all invariably must wear sneakers. Apparently, leather dress shoes are a no-no in this high-fashion group. Naturally, with a group like this, there are wheelchairs galore, and interestingly, a number of wheelchair pushers were jeans-clad middle-aged Indian women proudly displaying their airport ID badges around their necks. You could frequently hear, in unmistakable thick Gujarati accent, *"Aare harko, harko, you are blokeeng the pesej, harko. You are blind or whote?"* (Hey, move on. You are blocking the passage. Are you blind or what?) Public courtesy has never been our long suit in India.

INDIANS AS A GROUP

Over the years, I have traveled far, and I have traveled wide. At most airports in the world, as in most public places, there is an unwritten code of conduct; people generally respect authority and follow rules—except for my Indian brethren. My experience all over the world has brought me to realize that our people—Indians, resident or nonresident, educated or uneducated, rich or poor—cannot form a queue and board the way most other people do. We like to stand in groups. We do not like empty spaces, even a four-inch clearance between you and the next guy in front of you or behind you, if at all there is a line. Personal space is an unknown concept in India. After all, we are all friends, family, Indians, right? Our attitude is "We do not need to make a line, no matter what they announce. We can board as we please, not according to our seat number. We can push in as quickly as we can. No need to worry about the limitations on the number and size of carry-on luggage. Let us see what happens." One wonders how the same people who in private, personal life with family, friends, and acquaintances are perfect human beings, turn into wild cattle when dealing with strangers in public life.

Not just at the airports, bus stops, or train stations but in any public places as well, this behavior is the rule. There are at least two possible explanations.

First, this may well be a reflection of the residual pre-independence scarcity mentality of our grandparents under the British Raj—go get it before they run out of whatever there is to grab—or the constraints experienced by our parents during the post-independence license Raj or the fierce competition to get ahead of the other guy in today's upwardly mobile Indian society. This just shows basic personal insecurity and lack of confidence in the system.

Second, this is indicative of the cattle mentality not uncommon in developing countries. Masses cannot be wrong. If they are doing it, we can too. Ignorance follows ignorance. The fact that the private face of an individual may be quite different from his public face is explained beautifully by Friedrich Nietzsche. He says,

> Insanity in individuals is rare. But in groups, parties, nations and epochs, it is the rule.

From the Arab-Israeli conflict, to the Indo-Pakistani wars to the terrorists' hatred of America and its allies or from the rhetoric of the war of civilizations, to the security checkup procedures at airports, there is ample evidence of this group insanity everywhere.

At the Newark Airport, I saw in amazement that everyone seemed to accept such disorder as expected normal behavior from this particular group of my fellow Indian travelers. Nobody cared. Nobody was bothered. It seems difficult now, but some day, we will all realize that pushing and shoving serves no purpose, that there is a reserved seat for every passenger, and that the plane does not leave without having everybody on board. All passengers take off and land at the same time. And how hard is that to comprehend!

Once inside the plane, I noticed another fearless use of the ubiquitous Gujarati "*leng wage*" (language). Without batting an eye, one grandma fearlessly asked a gigantic African-American stewardess, "*Olu toy-late kya aagle chche?*" (Where is the toilet?). And lo and behold, the stewardess pointed her the right way. I guess if she has been on the EWR (Newark) to BOM (Mumbai) route a few times, she must speak fluent Gujarati.

Local politicians in India, who have painstakingly decimated all reference to Bombay replacing the name with Mumbai, must be agonizing over IATA's continued designation of Mumbai by the familiar abbreviation BOM. Perhaps using something like MUM or MOM instead might be more in line with regional pride.

THE FRIENDLY INDIAN

Once we took off, children resumed their running in the aisles to the great dismay of the stewardesses. Adult noise level built up as people settled down and relaxed. Once you open up and succumb to giving positive answers to assorted queries such as "*Oh, you are living (sic) in House Ton, no? You must be meeting my cousin brother, Jaggubhai Patel, no? He is living in America only,"* there are a lot more questions like *"May I kindly ask your good name, please?"* And after you have told them your good name, they continue,

> *How many issues (children) you are having?*
> *Are they married into good families?*
> *Are they having any issues?*
> *You must be earning big celery (salary) in America. May I kindly know how much it is?*
> *It must be too much, no? America is having so much richness.*

Indians are the friendliest, most talkative people in the world. Pretty soon, handbags opened up and *dhoklas, patras, and muthias* (Gujarati delicacies) started passing around. Indians known for their legendary tolerance will put up with anything—indescribable filth on the roads, crippling government bureaucracy, and absurd inconveniences except one thing, tasteless airline food. They must have their own. And they must generously share it with friends, neighbors, and fellow travelers.

A couple of rows in front of me, a kid cried nonstop for fourteen hours. After the first two hours, I almost squeezed his throat before I was overpowered by extreme empathy for his poor mother.

I did learn an important rule on this trip. Rule number 1 of traveling, on long trips with a group such as I was blessed with, finish all your restroom business within the first few hours of the trip when they are freshly cleaned and mostly unused. After that, it is an early introduction to the public restrooms in India known the world over for their stench and now some of them proudly displaying signs proclaiming *"Now Open for Business, Rs. 5:00 only, SULABH SHAUCHALAYA, inaugurated by the Honorable XYZ Ji, Chief MinisterJi on Diwali Day 2010."*

WELCOME TO THE NEW INDIA

This continental flight, nonstop to Mumbai, has certain advantages. It lands in Mumbai, unlike most other flights, at a very civilized hour of 9:30 PM, and at least currently, it is the only flight arriving at that time. That means there would be virtually no crowds at the airport, easy passage through immigration, rapid collection of bags, and quick exit. This concept in theory, worked remarkably well in practice too. Yes, India is changing. Whether that is enough to justify the much self-promoted and ballyhooed superpower status is highly questionable. The new international airport in Mumbai is indeed very spacious with a very large number of Newark-style arrival booths and the immigration and customs procedures are greatly simplified. Certain things, of course, do not change. One step out of the aircraft and my nostrils were filled with the unmistakable smell like, well, the smell of India.

In the past, the most painful thing, both for me and the immigration officer, used to be his one-finger typing of my majestic full name, Dnyanendrakumar Natwarlal Mayur. But no typing needed now. My passport got scanned in the same two seconds in which Joe Smith's got scanned. Immigration, bag collection, customs, currency exchange, and hiring a prepaid taxi took a total of thirty-five minutes. My flight was thirty minutes early, and I was sitting in the taxi at 9:35 PM. Never before have I landed in India at the civilized hour of 9:00 PM. It was always at the ungodly hour of 1:00 or 2:00 AM. Never before have I got out of the airport in thirty minutes. It was always a two—or three-hour affair.

Normally, this would have been a totally disorienting experience causing me to wonder where I had landed, except for the friendly comment of the immigration officer who greeted me with a warm "Welcome to Incredible India, how long will you be living?" I told him that I hoped I will be living for many more years, but my stay in India was going to be only about two months. He had ignored my wisecrack as he got busy placing his dinner order on his mobile *"Aare bola na, kushtomer khada hai, teen mutton samosa aur masala chai ekkis number booth. Jaldi karo"* (Didn't I tell you, my customer is waiting. Send three mutton samosas and spiced tea to Booth Number 21 right away). Certain things never change. I knew I was in India.

The cab ride from the airport to downtown took a full hour and gave me plenty of time to reflect on my flight, the people I observed in the plane, and the interesting experiences that lay ahead of me. But I could not get out of my mind the pushing and shoving and the general behavior of our people in public places—people apparently educated and well placed in life. Is this our culture? Is this mind-set an integral part of being Indian? And how will this play out as India aspires to be a global player, a major world power, and an attractive tourist center?

TWO

India Today

THE INDIA THAT IS

India has arrived on the global scene. In little over a decade, India has made major economic and technological strides. However, little progress has been made in the quality of life for its masses. There is not just one India, but as many Indias as one can imagine based on income, education, language, regional, and religious diversity. There are ten Cs that define modern India. They are communication, computers, construction, consumerism, culture, cricket, cinema, conspicuous consumption, corruption, and contrasting disparity. But the most important C that India needs is change.

Even a casual visitor returning to India after a short span of just a few years notices a dramatic change around him. The pride, optimism, and confidence in the walk and talk of young middle-class Indians and the vibrancy of its economy are unmistakable. You see, hear, and feel the energy and growing abundance around you. Economic boom of various magnitudes has come to many segments of the society. However, the eagerness to declare victory and euphoric celebration that a shining India has attained the successful nation status seems premature and may be nothing more than irrational exuberance. India represents a five-thousand-year-old ancient civilization with history, culture, and traditions like no other. Its population of 1.2 billion is the second largest in the world. And it is growing rapidly at the rate of nine million people per year.

Based on its nominal gross domestic product, GDP, of $1.6 trillion ($4 trillion on purchasing power parity, PPP, basis), India is the fourth largest economy. However, on the per capita basis, this GDP is a very sobering $1,370 ($3,500 PPP) making it 124th in the world. India's HDI (human development index—a combined normalized measure of life expectancy, literacy, and per capita GDP) also has a similar low rank of 128. India does have a very large pool of scientists and engineers, and it is the largest English-speaking nation. India likes to be considered a military superpower because of its continued development of nuclear capability and its 1.5 million strong, standing army, the third largest in the world.

Here are some reflections of an empathetic Indophile returning to his homeland for an extended stay after a long absence. Indeed, it has become fashionable to write about India these days, and there are books and articles galore written by a wide group of "experts" ranging from politicians, diplomats, foreign and domestic journalists, NRIs, and assorted real and pseudo intellectuals. However, these are my personal observations about the country, and I offer them without any pretense of erudite explanations, analyses, or solutions. The abysmal poverty, uncontrolled population growth, impossible traffic, and rampant corruption all over the country have been amply documented. I shall refrain from vividly describing any of those, for there is a lot more to the new India.

In my view, there are ten Cs that define modern India and even a cursory analysis of those reveals the nature of India's success. They are communication, computers, construction, consumerism, culture, cricket, cinema, conspicuous consumption, corruption, and contrasting disparity.

Politically and geographically, India is one country, but in a socioeconomic sense, there are many Indias. There is obscenely rich India, and there is abominably destitute India. There is pious, honest, God-fearing India; and there is shamelessly corrupt India. There is urban India, and there is rural India. There are Bollywood and NRI Indias. There is blatantly communal India, and there is sycophantic dynasty-worshipping India. There is geriatric political India that cannot think past octogenarian freedom fighters recycled the umpteenth time to their coveted ministerial "*kursees*" (chair or position) and there is bright-eyed youthful India 50 percent of whose population is below the age of twenty-five.

And then there is Tom Friedman's India. Friedman, of *The World Is Flat* fame, author and columnist for the *New York Times*, seems to believe seriously that the famed Infosys campus in Bangalore is India, that every kid in India is a math and science wizard, and that India is beating America's pants down in every sphere of technical activity.

The present status and future potential of each of these Indias are markedly different. Here are the factors that define India today.

COMMUNICATION

Communication represents one of the most dramatic and visible changes in today's India. There are over five hundred million cell phone (called mobiles here) users and more than seven to eight million are being added monthly. By some estimates, the total will be over six hundred million cell phones in a year. This means that one in two Indians will have a cell phone. This is particularly remarkable because until 1990, the Indian telephone system was simply pathetic with only about eight to nine million utterly unreliable land lines, and it took God's (or a politician's, which is the same thing in India) special blessings to get one.

Today, a typical middle-class Indian child, like his (her) Western counterpart, is born with a cell phone attached to the ear. Before he learns to talk, his fingers are adept at SMSing "Madhuri u r gr8." The phone plans are inexpensive with quality and coverage better than those in most places in the world and just about everybody, from minor shopkeepers to taxi drivers to the corner *paanwallas* (vendors of a certain leaf and condiments that Indians chew on after a meal), has one. But there is an annoying downside to this. Indians seem to be excessively obsessed with phones, messaging and phone conversing generally without regard to others around them. Frequent disturbance by ringing mobile phones is common in concert halls, movie theaters, and even during formal meetings.

COMPUTERS AND OTHER HIGH-TECH INDUSTRIES

Computers and information technology (IT) in general have been the drivers of India's economic growth. That, together with India's very large pool of English-speaking professionals and low-wage rates, has caused an influx of multinationals like Amex, AIG, HP, Sun, Dell, IBM, SAP, Intel, Microsoft, Oracle, TI, GE, GM, Caterpillar, DuPont, and Eli Lilly, just to name a few, among the over one hundred multinational corporations. They occupy glossy industrial parks mushrooming in cities like Mumbai, Delhi, Bangalore, and Hyderabad. Pune has become the Detroit of India. According to McKinsey, India's IT revenues are about one hundred billion dollars, and the industry employs over one million people. In Bangalore itself, there are about one hundred fifty thousand IT professionals.

The growth of high-tech industry is promoting a reverse brain drain. The Bollywood film *Swadesh* depicted national pride and patriotism as the catalysts for the emerging trend of the great homeward march of the Indian diaspora. There is work to be done at home, and there are better opportunities to get bigger jobs and go higher, sooner. A 2009 Harvard study projects that over one hundred thousand NRIs will return from the US to India over the next five years. Most major IT companies estimate that up to 10 percent of applications they receive for management positions are from NRIs.

This is a very heartening trend. Overseas Indians are returning not just for emotional or patriotic reasons but for economic and market reasons as well, and that is a true sign of the arrival of India on the international scene. The challenge, of course, would be to streamline the resettling process by removing bureaucratic obstacles and improving the overall business climate in India.

However, even more impressive than IT may be the growth and self-sufficiency of India's agro industry. In 1968, India imported nine million metric tons of food grains. Forty years later, in 2008, it had a surplus of some sixty million tons. Other notable businesses in India are diamond exports with over eight billion dollars in annual revenue and garments, a twenty-billion dollar industry. India's foreign exchange reserves have increased from near zero in the early 1990s to 120 billion dollars today. However, as mentioned earlier, the totality of India's economic activity amounts to a per capita GDP of only about $1,370, a figure that is still among the lowest in the world.

CONSTRUCTION

The most dominant symbol of the changing India and its economic boom is its new industrial parks and apartment buildings mushrooming in urban areas at a pace unprecedented in history. To its credit, the country has embarked on a program of certain much-needed construction of national highways, expressways, flyovers in major cities, and special projects like the Bandra-Worli Sea Link in Mumbai or the Konkan Railway in the state of Maharashtra, just as examples. And yet, in view of the size of the country's population and its current and projected needs, much more is needed to be done in the whole infrastructure arena.

Apartment houses of all shapes and sizes—some ugly, some elegant—seem to be rising up overnight to meet the insatiable demand. Much of this growth seems sporadic and is frequently without the necessary infrastructure of roads and utilities with the inevitable consequences of congestion, traffic jams, pollution, and water and power shortages. An even bigger consequence is the phenomenal spurt in land and housing prices which, in some parts of cities like Mumbai, are considered to be the highest in the world ahead of New York, London, Tokyo, and Moscow.

There are a couple of explanations for this paradox of absurdly high real estate prices in one of the poorest countries. The remittances from the NRIs in the Middle East, Asia, Europe, and the USA have been partly responsible for this jump. However, the real reason behind this is the undeclared, unaccounted for "black" money. In Indian politics, corruption and construction are synonyms. Almost always, any land/housing transaction is based on a 40/60 formula—40 percent in cash (black money) and 60 percent in legal checks. India's parallel economy of this underground, undeclared tax-free money is reportedly bigger than its legitimate economy. It is shocking but not surprising that in a country of well over a billion people, only about thirty-five million pay substantial income taxes.

CONSUMERISM

The growing wealth is converting India into a consumer society. However, of the population of 1.2 billion, only about 25 percent or three hundred million fall in the categories of middle class or the wealthy class with family incomes sufficiently high enabling them to afford Western goods and prices. The other 75 percent can consume only locally produced, cheaper goods. The relative youth of the Indian population brings in its own unique dynamic to the socioeconomic scene. Gigantic shopping malls are springing up in major cities in numbers that may be unsustainable. But for now, Indians with any money at all are crowding the malls to shop, to socialize, to eat at food courts featuring KFCs and McDonald's, or just to walk around and pass time.

Mostly everything that is available in a typical mall in the US is now available in India and at almost equal prices in dollar terms. TV channels and glossy magazines overflow with ads for brand-name products—Toyota Camry's; Ray-Ban glasses; Sony electronics; Nike shoes; Kellogg's cereals; and Johnny Walker red, black, and blue labels. But once again, there are multiple Indias within India, and what applies to urban India is quite different from what applies to rural India. Places like Mumbai and Delhi boast some of the finest restaurants in the world with hospitality and service to match. But the most impressive, colorful, and visible exposition of India's new consumerism is in the apparel industry and particularly in women's clothing. Just walk into a sari shop and check out the hustle-bustle, the variety of styles and fashions, and the panorama of brilliant colors, the richness of fabrics, and the enthusiasm of the salesman. Exclusive shops or street-side vendors all are fully stocked. Those who can afford it eat, dress, and live very well in India.

In the changing India, an amusing and at times bothersome fact is that the upwardly mobile Indians, especially the young generation, have jumped with both feet into the American bandwagon. They seem to be hallucinating of being Americans themselves adopting American vocabulary (mainly the slang), American foods and fads, American-brand clothing, and aspiring the American lifestyle with emphasis on individualism, privacy, personal transportation, and social customs celebrating even obscure American traditions like Halloween and St. Valentine's Day! I think it is rather late in the game for such blind worship especially now when the West is generally looking to the East for wisdom and salvation.

CULTURE

Indian culture with its traditions, religions, and rituals makes it one of the most enigmatic countries in the world. The rites of birth, death, and weddings remain exceedingly important to an average family. In the urban middle class, education is king. In addition, there is considerable interest in the performing arts of music, dance, theater, and literature. Indian philosophy, spiritualism, and the wisdom of its ancient sages and scholars are recognized with great admiration by intellectuals all over the world. Indians are generally very proud of their culture and religious teachings.

Unfortunately, more often than not, this sense of personal pride does not extend to public behavior, social awareness, or civic responsibility. Quest for money continues and nepotism flourishes. An inherent sense of scarcity has led to an exaggerated survival instinct as manifested in shoving and pushing to get ahead in any line, be it at the bank or airport, movies, or train stations.

India remains an essentially feudal and exploitative society with master-servant relationships well established and understood in most interactions. Servitude to any figure of authority is evident in the stunningly common use of "sir" or the Indian appendix "ji" for anybody in power. At the same time, rudeness, arrogance, and discourtesy to subordinates and "servants" are quite common. The capitalistic societies of the West seem to be far more egalitarian and socially conscious than India despite India's avowed socialism.

On a personal level, the average Indian is friendly, hospitable, honest, undemanding, fatalistic, pious, and highly family-oriented. But above all, he is very tolerant—tolerant of bureaucratic malfeasance, daily inconveniences, and stinking public restrooms, incredible filth on the roads, corrupt politicians, social injustice, and unfairness. But Indians are a hardy and resilient lot. No trauma or hindrance is bad enough. Life goes on in spite of eight-hours-a-day power outages, water scarcity, bad commutes to work, and politicians routinely swindling crores of rupees in public funds.

People make themselves happy by finding solace in small pleasures, religious festivals, favorite TV serials, *masala chai and pakoras* (spicy tea and a snack), neighborly gossip, and high-decibel talk about cricket and politics. I am awed by the Indian masses. Despite all odds, they make India run. The Indian people are known for their service culture, the warmth and the personal touch, and the world-famous bobble head, a respectful indication of acceptance and agreement with whomever they happen to be talking with. Domestic help in India is almost always very good and so is the service from repairmen, delivery personnel, and others although keeping a time commitment or even showing up at all as agreed can be a challenge.

CRICKET

Cricket in India is much more than a sport. It is a religion, and the local cricketers are worshipped as deities. Even in sports-crazy and super affluent America, no sport and no athlete, not even the likes of Michael Jordan or Tiger Woods, come even close to their counterparts in the Indian cricket world in adulation and material rewards bestowed on them. India has recently launched professional cricket leagues with mercenaries hired from all over the world and duly equipped with pom-pom cheer girls trained by American professional teams. Loud, animated talk of cricket and politics dominates male conversation in all social settings. Indians live, sleep, eat, drink, talk, argue over, and watch either cricket or politics whenever they can.

CINEMA AND OTHER ENTERTAINMENT

Bollywood, India's version of Hollywood (shouldn't it be Mollywood, after Mumbai? Surely, this calls for a strike) enjoys prestige, status, and popularity like no other human enterprise. India has perfected the technology of making Bollywood girls pretty, glitzy, and glamorous. India produces upward of eight hundred flashy and extravagant movies a year. While most of the movies follow an extremely predictable set formula of escapism, a small class of the movies called "art cinema" or "parallel cinema" is quite good.

To succeed as a movie star, there are certain basic requirements. Just as in Indian politics, dynasty rules in the movie industry. With a famous family name, you are a shoe-in even before your birth. Next, you must be skilled in Hinglish (mixture of Hindi and English) where you randomly alternate between English and Hindi mostly saying the same thing in English after you have said it partially first in Hindi, or vice versa, typically in incomplete sentences strewn with "you know's" and "na."

Finally, "macho mania" prevails, so if you are a male, you must pump iron and bare your chest a few times in the movie regardless of need, and if you are a female, you must do a pelvis-thrusting dance a few times celebrating whatever reason or occasion you can think of. India has now run out of places to dance in so the preferable locations for this activity have now moved overseas as in front of the Sydney Opera House, the Eiffel Tower in Paris, or Big Ben in London. Propelled by their national recognition and fame, Indian movie stars are now invading the very ripe arena of Indian politics. There is a lot more money to be made in politics, which requires much less work and no specific qualifications.

In the broader world of entertainment, Indian TV boasts a large number of channels in all regional languages. Indian serials command a very loyal audience and have developed their own feel-good escapist formula involving traditional joint family of super wealthy businessmen, the family duly equipped with one angel "*bahoo*" (daughter-in-law) and another real villain, all immaculately dressed and loaded with tons of jewelry at all hours of the day conspiring away in their fabulous palatial residences. Indeed, there is a bright side too. The advent and popularity of TV has been a great boon to traditional Indian performing arts—particularly dance and music. Wonderful shows like *Sa Re Ga Ma* are produced and telecast in many languages and give a great opportunity and exposure to aspiring and talented youth.

It is a joy to read the newspapers in India if you can get past the acronyms. Indians love acronyms and politics provide a great opportunity for their use. BJP, RJD, BSP, RSS, DMK, CM, PM, CMO, PMO, CWG, HC, SC, RBI, SEBI, JRD, SRK, JEE, SIT, HRD, JAB, PIL, IPL, ODI, LBW, RTI, MNC, and the like are very common; and you are just supposed to know them. But beyond these hundreds of standard abbreviations, they also create new ones on the run as in "our ED makes our customers very happy." This *ED* is not what the Viagra generation might think it is—erectile dysfunction. No, ED here, of course, is *environmental design*, a natural for the modern green India. How can you not know it? Here is another gem of a headline:

> "I-T probe links deal with Rs 425 crore FP paid to WSG by MSM
> for IPL media rights." Wow! No kidding, whatever this means.

In the West, and particularly the US, the newspapers are an excuse for advertisements and sales promotions and a chronology of local murders and rapes (foreign lands do not exist unless the US is involved in a military action there). Unlike them, Indian newspapers, especially those of national stature, have excellent news coverage—domestic and international, opinion columns, and sports and entertainment items in addition to interesting tidbits.

CONSPICUOUS CONSUMPTION

Despite all the talk about Gandhian simplicity and equality, India seems to be a country of the privileged, run by the privileged, and for the benefit of the privileged. Conspicuous consumption is the order of the day. "The bigger, the better" mantra rules life. From Bollywood stars to politicians to business owners, there is a display of obscene, unconscionable wealth at every possible opportunity, be it an event like an engagement, birthday, or wedding or exhibition of personal residences, hobbies, or passions. In socialistic India, the super rich are the modern-day kings given to the same extravagance of royalty. From time to time, stories about the fabulous lifestyles of the Indian glitterati show up in the newspapers and make interesting reading. The following excerpt from a news item in the *Times of India* gives an idea. Here is one about industrialist Vijay Mallya, he of the Kingfisher fame, whose beer and the elegant UB City in Bangalore are among public favorites:

> That the flamboyant chairman of the UB group, likes the good life is well known. His penchant for fast cars, castles, horses, jets, yachts and game lodges is well chronicled. It looks as if islands are his latest passion. The buzz in Bangalore is that he has bought an island in Europe, ostensibly off the coast of Monte Carlo . . . Mallya's lifestyle—the sheer scale and lavishness of it—leaves most bedazzled. He has houses around the globe, castles in Scotland, town houses in London, Monte Carlo, Manhattan, Sausalito and innumerable properties in India . . . His three yachts, his four private jets, his 240-strong vintage car fleet, his Force India Formula 1 team and thoroughbreds not to mention the Porsches, Bentleys, Maseratis & Ferraris make him one of the most colorful Indians.

(In late 2011, Mallya's Kingfisher Airline was reported to be in deep financial trouble.)

Maybe, there is nothing wrong with this. "If you got it, flaunt it" goes the saying. There are ultra-rich people all over the world, and if individuals like Mallya have earned what they have, they can do what they want with their wealth. It is just that such luxurious lifestyle seems to be at odds with the conditions in the rest of the country. One might be tempted to rule out the much publicized billion-dollar home of Ambani or Mallya's lifestyle as mere aberrations. Not so. Every Indian of whatever background or education seems to aspire to this feudal lifestyle and worshipping creature comforts of all sorts.

The lifestyle of three hundred million people in India's middle and upper class is supported by nine hundred million people, the "have-nots" of India. They cook, clean, wash, sweep, garden, drive, and babysit for them. Most upper-class households are dependent upon an army of servants and *ayahs* (maids). This upper-class group will be totally dysfunctional without them. Mahatma Gandhi, the revered father of this nation, who warned us against the following seven sins, must be turning in his grave for most of India's privileged classes specialize in just these:

- Wealth without work
- Pleasure without conscience
- Knowledge without character
- Commerce without morality
- Science without humanity
- Worship without sacrifice
- Politics without principle

CORRUPTION

Recently, in the news all over the nation has been a spate of high-level corruption cases both in the public and private sectors—the Adarsh Housing scam, 2G spectrum distribution, the Commonwealth Games, just to name a few. Corruption by politicians with enormous authority and access to taxpayer fund is nothing new in the public sector in India. However, the private sector can do it too, and the bigger they get, the greater is the opportunity. A glaring example of this is Satyam computers, which a couple of years ago carried out a fraud as massive and as blatant as Enron's in the US. Its shenanigans, among the greatest in Indian corporate history, caused a collective loss to the investors of over five billion dollars. India's motto, proudly displayed everywhere, is "Satyameva Jayate" meaning truth alone wins. In today's India, truth has been replaced by fraud.

Certainly, corruption exists at various levels and in various degrees in almost all countries of the world with few exceptions, if any. Even the successful and affluent democracies like the US or Japan are not immune. However, in most civilized nations, it is confined to isolated, massive, and one-of-a-kind occurrences; the average citizen is almost never impacted. Not so in India.

On a daily basis, India confronts corruption at all levels and in most activities; and real estate and infrastructure, the bulwarks of the new economy, present the greatest opportunity. Politicians and middlemen, in a position to sign and approve your legitimate request, insist on huge bribes before doing anything. Unprincipled leaders are India's biggest scourge. While India is lauded as the world's biggest democracy, it is noteworthy that no less than 113 of the 543 members of India's Parliament have criminal cases pending against them!

The pervasive corruption has attained a very high profile and almost official status in the most unlikely arena, higher education in the professional fields. Because of the extreme inadequacy of seats available in traditional government-sponsored engineering and medical schools, private entrepreneurs backed by politicians have moved in aggressively establishing colleges and universities all over the country with admissions for sale at prices that make the middle class shiver. Getting your daughter married and your son admitted to college are the biggest, most expensive, most anxiety-causing propositions for Indian parents today.

CONTRASTING DISPARITY

Two-thirds of India's population lives in its 660,000 villages where even basic sanitation, electricity, and water supply are not guaranteed. This is a far cry from the pockets of affluent areas in the metropolitan cities that are comparable to any of the best neighborhoods in the West. India is truly a land of contrasts and paradoxes. The images of computers being hauled in bullock carts or kids defecating roadside by the house with a cell phone in the hand are quite common and well-publicized. In India we have computers; just don't ask for drinking water. We have cars; we just don't have roads or parking places. The disparity between the rich and poor is mind-boggling. The view of India from inside the Taj Mahal Hotel is quite different from that from Dharavi, the largest slum in the world that packs one million destitute people in a square mile of subhuman living conditions. Here is a news report from New Delhi dated November 14, 2011.

India remains the "dirtiest and filthiest" country in the world; Rural Development Minister Jairam Ramesh said today. During an interaction with the audience, he continued, "I am concerned. The biggest challenge I am facing, is to educate people about sanitation. Sixty per cent of all open defecation in the world is in India. Today, in many parts of India, you have women with a mobile phone, going out to answer the call of nature. I mean it is paradoxical . . . you have a mobile phone and you don't have a toilet. When you have a toilet, you don't use the toilet, use it as a ware-house," he said.

The India depicted in Zee TV serials today is quite different from that in Satyajit Ray's realistic movies in the past. While the movie *Slumdog Millionaire* is fiction, sadly in India, slums are real and there are lots of them; and millionaires are real, and there are lots of them. The corruption and lawlessness shown in the movie are also real, ever so increasing the gap between the rich and the poor by creating more slums, by creating newer millionaires and billionaires. India is thriving and failing simultaneously. On the one hand, one sees elite arcades with shops selling Milanese fashions, Waterford crystal, latest electronic gadgetry, $25,000 worth of diamonds, and Godiva chocolates to the rich and famous. On the other hand, nearly half of all under five-year-olds here suffer from malnutrition.

India is a country of extremes—that of monumental poverty and a small wealthy elite group. It has the largest number of billionaires in Asia and has more than one hundred thousand millionaires. But the disparity between the rich and the poor is growing wider. Exclusive high-rises sprout next to shanty towns. Abysmal slums surround glittering malls. The poor salute and serve the wealthy. Social thinkers understand and warn that India cannot claim to be a progressive leader in the community of nations with its high levels of poverty and malnutrition, and political scientists predict that violence could break out and spread if inequalities are not reduced quickly.

In this changing India, most of the change has been for people who were wealthy to begin with. The rich get richer, the poor get babies. For the have-nots, life seems very much the same with very little to look forward to. In the middle of rising wealth in selected sections of the society, the hungry children tapping on the windows of cars stalled in traffic jams is a sad reminder that the jubilation over the wishful chanting of "India superpower" is quite premature.

No other land in the world has the dichotomies that India presents, the extreme dualities that coexist here. You feel proud and ashamed, good and bad, happy and sad, optimistic and pessimistic about this place all at the same time. You love the beauty of the culture and the simplicity of the people; you hate the bureaucracy and corruption. You admire the intelligence and hard work and pride of some. You despise the blatant exploitation of the masses and the servant system, the religious and social hypocrisy, and the insensitivity to others.

In summary, it is clear that India is a land of ultimate contrasts. One can say anything about India. It will be true. And so will be the exact opposite. Efficiency and chaotic disorder, secularism and fanaticism, obscene wealth and total destitution, Gandhian nonviolence and mafia's murderous frenzy, virtue and vice, exploitation and charity, piety and vulgarity, selfless social activists and corrupt public figures, hope and despair—that is India today. Because there are so many Indias within India, it cannot be but complex. And complexity can breed crises. It is to India's credit that it has awakened and is struggling to lift itself up, slowly shedding the historic shackles of the caste system for a culture of high-tech enterprise, Bollywood, cricket, VIPs and VVIP celebrities in movies, business, and politics.

India today—interesting, yes; fascinating, yes; confusing, yes. Of wonderful people, exotic food, beautiful arts, and a rich culture, yes. And yet *"Mera Bharat Mahan"* (my India is great) is a meaningless slogan, at least for now. It can be *Mahan* (great) with the eleventh *C—C* for *change*, as discussed in the sequel to this essay, "India Tomorrow."

(An earlier version of this essay was serialized in Voice of Asia*)*

THREE

India Tomorrow

THE INDIA THAT CAN BE

India is a land of enormous potential. This article is a futuristic look about what India can be. It must draw on its incomparable resources—the energy of its young population of today and the wisdom of its ancient sages. India was once a land of great wealth, profound knowledge, and rich culture. It can be restored to that old glory by taking a holistic approach based on traditional values and wisdom adapted to the modern times. As Niccolo Machiavelli once said, "There is nothing more necessary to a community than the prestige it had at the outset."

The last essay entitled "India Today" outlined the ten *C*s that define present-day India and discussed the nature of India's recent economic progress. Among the ten *C*s, communication, computers, and construction are clear positives. Consumerism, cultural issues, cricket, and cinema are invariant facts of life in India. Conspicuous consumption, corruption, and contrasting disparity are serious negatives. That essay represents the facts as they seem to appear today. Tomorrow is unknown, and what it will bring is unpredictable. But there are no constraints on what India can be.

India has enormous potential, and what it can achieve is limitless. This essay presents a fearless peek into tomorrow's India. It is a dream. It is an India-lover's fantasy based on some unmistakable trends—the success of individuals of Indian origin all over the world in a diversity of fields; the increasing global recognition and popularity of distinctly Indian specialties like Yoga, Ayurveda, Bollywood dance, and Tandoori cooking; the focus of Indian children on higher education; the increasing wealth, enterprise, and confidence of Indian youth; general awareness of the nation's problems as well as its strengths within India; and the recognition of its potential outside.

The fact that today's India is short on the infrastructure of roads, airports, and utilities is well-known and amply discussed by numerous authors. But with a national will, planning, and discipline, these can be fixed in a relatively short period of time. What is going for India, even in its current state of poverty, is its large base of skilled, English-speaking professionals and its strength in the form of its democratic institutions and independent judiciary. These, coupled with its unique demography, can catapult India into a truly great nation of tomorrow if its pervasive corruption and the incredible disparity between the rich and the poor can be controlled, if not fully eliminated. Certainly, these are big ifs, but all this is in the realm of possibility and can happen in a decade or two. It can be brought about by making the most of India's demographic advantage, avoiding the mistakes of the West, being truly Indian, cleaning up politics, and leveraging education.

It is hardly a secret that India has many assets. It is a land of perpetual sunshine and fertile plains. It is self-sufficient in food, and it has ample mineral resources. It has a long coastline, impressive mountains, and a network of rivers. It has a solid foundation of spirituality and the eternal wisdom of its saints and sages from times immemorial covering all aspects of human activity. However, none of these great assets is as impressive as the unique demographic advantage that India may be able to exploit in the near future.

MAKING MOST OF THE DEMOGRAPHIC ADVANTAGE

Today, 50 percent of India's population is below the age of twenty-five, making this oldest land the youngest country in the world. This is the most positive aspect of India's future because the rest of the world is rapidly aging. According to the United Nations, in a few decades, the largest group in India will be that of the forty—to fifty-year-olds, the most productive years of human beings. In contrast, the most populated group will be that of the fifty-five—to sixty-five-year-olds in countries like China, Japan, USA, and Europe. They will have an excessive number of retirees relative to and being supported by a much smaller working population. The young have the flexibility to adapt, absorb, conceptualize, and innovate. They are optimistic, energetic, and enthusiastic. Even today, the Indian youth, regardless of the economic strata, is focused on education and is getting more and more comfortable with the use of technology.

As these young people grow up, get educated, trained, and experienced, it is not inconceivable that India tomorrow will be teeming with armies of computer-savvy professionals, adept at advanced communication techniques, working in global teams on problems of energy, environment, banking, space, and medicine. In this dream-world, India could have the largest, most qualified, most productive, and diverse workforce of any nation, any time in history. Demographic trends are long-lasting and not easily reversed. This augurs well for India.

AVOIDING THE MISTAKES OF THE WEST

India tomorrow will be an enlightened nation. It will have recognized that you can never be a winner, never be number 1, or a leader in anything simply by imitating others. It will have stopped trying to be like America or any other country. It will have learned from the mistakes of the West. It will have learned that American-style, free-for-all capitalism has no guarantees of success for all, its benefits can be ephemeral; it is sometimes fueled by uncontrolled greed and, more often than not, can breed fraudulent businesses and selfish executives. It will have learned that for the most part, the Western business model, family unit, and unabashed pursuit of individualism are not inclusive of all citizens and thus have certain inherent problems. It will have learned that "it takes a village" for any successful human enterprise and that the state does have a role to play in ensuring the society's well-being.

Americans proudly say that their system is a great experiment. The last decade has proved beyond doubt that the American socioeconomic experiment has many flaws. On the other hand, Western democracies, particularly the American system, have several positives in the form of individual freedoms, openness to other cultures and new ideas, and certain social safety nets (like Medicare, social security, unemployment benefits) that are worth absorbing by any aspiring nation. In this dream-world, India tomorrow will have leapfrogged over all the trials and errors of other countries, avoiding their mistakes but building on their successes on its path of becoming a fair and advanced society.

POLITICAL GOLDEN MEAN

Tomorrow's new India rejects the self-indulgent capitalism while recognizing that pure socialism fails to provide adequate motivation and incentive essential for progress. It believes that success is a product of the society we live in, that certain cultural values are instrumental in individual success, and that genetic factors are conducive to development of skills. Keeping this in mind, the new Indian state will provide the environment for success to all its citizens. The traditional Indian culture is far more suited to family, team, and society orientation than to Western-style, highly competitive, every-one-for-himself individualism. So India tomorrow will avoid the extremes of capitalism as well as socialism settling at a golden mean where both the state and individual citizens have well-defined, appropriate responsibilities toward each other. Having learned from the mistakes of other countries, the new India will pay special attention to issues of family values, transportation, media, waste minimization, and entertainment.

PUBLIC TRANSPORTATION

Currently India has the largest network of railroad in the world. This will be further expanded and revamped to provide inexpensive, clean, safe, comfortable, and reliable intercity transportation. India will have recognized that excessive dependence on personal car, be it a cheap Maruti or an expensive Lexus, is just not the right cost-effective solution for the conditions in India.

India will have learned that when it was flirting with making cheaper cars like the Nano available to a large number of aspiring Indians, many Western countries, burned by high energy prices, were clamoring for more public transportation and exploring the ways of weaning themselves away from their auto addiction. Tomorrow's India will have the best technologically advanced, alternative-fuel-based, environmentally friendly public transportation systems.

SELF-MONITORING PRESS

India will have an independent and vigorous press; however, the limits and problems of unbridled coverage will be recognized. Once hailed as a major innovation, the twenty-four-hour news with its muckraking, focus on trivia, and constant bombardment of the same news regardless of its significance does more harm than good. In India tomorrow, the enlightened media will actively monitor itself without the need for government intervention.

WASTE MINIMIZATION

A possible consequence of the increasing wealth is rising consumerism and waste of which the United States is a living monument. Americans like everything big. Their houses, cars, public places, and consumption patterns all emphasize bigness. Perhaps this was considered the beauty and the strength of America—that there was no shortage of anything, that they could afford to use as much as they wanted, spend as much as was needed. However, such an approach is frequently wasteful and is now proving to be unsustainable. Fortunately, in general, most Indians are quite frugal by nature. That is a virtue that will be retained in the new India despite its increasing standard of living. As a matter of policy, India will be conscious of the optimal use of its resource and environmental conservation.

THE RIGHT PLACE OF SPORTS AND ENTERTAINMENT

Indians are fun-loving people, and they take their sports, particularly cricket, and Bollywood seriously. In a free and progressive society, entertainment and creative performing arts have a definite role to play. But it is always a supporting role. With increasing affluence, there is a danger of this role growing out of proportion, becoming an end in itself as it has now happened in some of the Western countries. For example, reports after reports point to the decline of competitiveness and academic achievement by high school students in certain parts of the world. Among other reasons, one of the most important causes of this situation is obsession with spectator sports, music, video games, TV, movies, and worship of highly compensated athletes or entertainers who, more often than not, are poor role models for the young people. Further, it turns children into lazy dreamers interested in get-rich-quick schemes. The lure of easy money and unrealistic expectations destroys motivation and work ethic.

India tomorrow will keep entertainment and sports in perspective and the Indian children will never lose their advantage in math and science and will actually build up their lead in other areas of study.

FAMILY VALUES

The core of any society is the family unit. Cultural, religious, and moral education starts at home. Ethical and patriotic values are taught and developed at home. In most cases, personality and behavior problems start at home and thus can be solved within the family. Traditional Indian culture is family-centered. In the changing world of today, the family system comes under the greatest pressure. Two-career families, latchkey children growing up with TV and video games and the aggressive pursuit of personal gratification can take a heavy toll on the family. In India tomorrow, public policy and social systems will be refocused on the family with special considerations for childcare, women's rights, and equality issues. Women will have attained total parity with men in every aspect of life.

BEING TRULY INDIAN

In India tomorrow, Indians will be proud of themselves, their country, their culture, and their languages. They will be true Indians, preferring Indian food, arts, books, music, and movies to Western alternatives. India has a very rich heritage of classical music, dance, literature, and theater. In the new India, these will be generously supported, proudly promoted, and nurtured like never before. Indians will proudly return to *back to the basics,* holistic approach to a virtuous life recommended by the wise sages of ancient India. This approach encompasses pious thinking and spirituality, unity and harmony with nature, performing arts for the uplifting of the mind, yoga for peace and fitness, naturopathy and Ayurveda for health, and Indian vernacular architecture for shelters that are organic and sustainable. Interestingly, many of the contemporary Western thinkers are seeing the wisdom of the Indian sages before Indians discover it. And as demonstrated by the remarkable popularity of yoga everywhere, the world is moving toward all things Indian, including mutton samosas and Bollywood dances. There is much that India can teach the rest of humanity.

RELIGION

Indian scriptures contain profound wisdom and spiritual teachings. India has always been considered a religious country. However, much of the prevalent practice of religion is an unenlightened, ritual-based, blind-faith exercise. A classic example of this is the frequent recasting of politicians like Indira and Sonia Gandhi in the images of goddesses Durga or Kali. Similarly, most of the claims of spirituality tend to be fads promoted by foreign visitors who, within a week of visiting some ashram in a corner of India, suddenly discover divine spirituality, write a book, and return back to the life they came from. In India tomorrow, the Indian scriptures will be studied seriously and formally for the incomparable knowledge and understanding they provide about the self and the universe. The study of Sanskrit will be supported, encouraged, and promoted. Of course, India will remain a secular country drawing on the strengths of Hinduism and its distinguishing characteristics of tolerance and acceptance of all faiths as opposed to the fanaticism of others that has caused so much misery in human history.

AYURVEDA AND YOGA

Health-care concerns and costs are among the most important in a family budget. While research in Western medicine is progressing very rapidly all over the world, it has its limitations. It is very expensive, and most of the times, its emphasis is on curing the symptom. A major malady of the health-care system in the developed world is its cost because of the many middlemen involved and the fact that it has become a major profit-making business for hospitals, insurance companies, drug makers, and doctors.

In a civilized country that genuinely cares for all its citizens, the noble callings of health care and education should never be profit-making businesses. They should be considered essential services that the state provides to everybody as they do in much of Western Europe and, particularly, in Scandinavia. India tomorrow will adopt this nonprofit approach to service delivery. Further, for medicine itself, India will draw on its time-honored alternative of Ayurveda that focuses on lifestyle changes and can effectively complement Western medicine. Formal study and practice of Ayurveda and Yoga will find its rightful place in educational curricula.

Historian Will Durant says India was the cradle of civilization and gave the world man's finest intellectual systems—mathematics, the decimal system, grammar, chess, and philosophy. Today, the world has aggressively adopted another one of India's great contributions, Yoga. The word comes from the Sanskrit root meaning "to yoke" or to unite, to unite with nature. It trains one to harmonize posture, breathing, and thinking in order to attain peace with self and harmony with surroundings. This union makes the body free of disease and the mind free of negative thought. Given the well-known fact that more than 80 percent of the illnesses have psychosomatic origins, a genuine practice of Yoga has real transformative power over today's stressful life.

INDIAN VERNACULAR ARCHITECTURE

Vernaculus, in Latin, means domestic, native, or indigenous. Indian vernacular architecture has been recognized as one of the best climate-responsive forms. It seeks to establish a rapport between the universe and the chosen terrain for the building. Vernacular, by definition, is suitable for the local context and is sustainable. It is instinct-inspired, minimalist, informal, and functional. It is found in rural India devoid of urban sophistication. Built by local people, for local people, with natural local materials, it has no frills or unnecessary decorations.

As opposed to the Vernacular, Polite architecture is characterized by stylistic elements intentionally incorporated in the design for aesthetic purposes. Along with climate, geography, and materials, the techniques adopted in vernacular architecture are also a reflection of history, environment, local culture, traditions, craftsmanship, and human behavior. The age-old vernacular structures seen in parts of India today have withstood the test of time. They demonstrate the proven techniques based on centuries of experience and wisdom of Indian architects.

Vernacular architecture responds to the extremes of Indian climates by thoughtful physical designs for water channels, terraces, pillared halls, courtyards, intricate grills, *Zarokhas* (clerestory window) all specifically adopted for local weather conditions. Examples of innovative natural air-conditioning abound in palaces built three or four hundred years ago in India.

Currently, there is a global frenzy of green-thinking and sustainable development in response to ozone depletion and global warming. The current concepts of energy conservation, wind and solar power did not exist in the past. But the Indian architects knew. They were way ahead of their times as evidenced by their simple, functional, and comfortable shelters built in style that was organic and sustainable. In India tomorrow, the environment-friendly techniques of vernacular architecture will be formally studied, further developed, and adapted to modern times and technology for use in various parts of India and elsewhere.

DEVELOPING TOURISM

The India of tomorrow will be the world's biggest center of tourism. From the heavenly gardens of Kashmir to Vivekananda's Kanyakumari, from the majestic Himalayas to the mighty Indian Ocean, from the dense rain forests of Assam to the endless pristine deserts of Jaisalmer, the vast expanse of India covers every kind of terrain and weather in regions of unsurpassed natural beauty. And then there is its five-thousand-year-old history with majestic palaces, formidable forts, and ornate temples surrounded by the panorama of its various cultures, costumes, customs, and culinary specialties. Today, much of all this is visible through glossy color pictures and brochures, videos, and documentaries promoted by the government in its "Incredible India" campaigns. What these beautiful pictures do not show is the pushing and shoving, the smells and sounds, the routine discomforts and inconveniences that are so India today.

In India tomorrow, Indian tourism's full potential will be realized as places are cleaned up, procedures streamlined, adequate infrastructure developed, and total attention is focused on the comforts of the tourists as the guests of the nation. India will set new global standards for service and comfort in tourism.

CLEANING UP POLITICS

The most dramatic change in the fantasy world of India tomorrow will be in the political arena. India will have recognized that unscrupulous, corrupt politicians have been the worst scourge of the nation. It will have been recognized that the much-touted value of geriatric experience was among the most overrated things in India. This change was precipitated during the 2009 national elections when an octogenarian pitted himself against the incumbent septuagenarian for the coveted prime ministership as the harbinger of change! This in the youngest country with the second largest population in the world! Contrast this with the then-new US president, forty-seven-year-old Obama, and his potential challenger in the future, Bobby Jindal, thirty-seven and of Indian descent.

Indian philosophy defines four distinct phases of life broken into twenty-five-year segments. The first, *Brahmacharyashram,* is for education and building your life's foundation; the second, from age twenty-five to fifty, *Grihasthashram,* is the most productive period and is for raising the family and working to contribute to the society. The third quarter from age fifty on is *Wanprasthashram* for gradual retirement, and the final quarter from age seventy-five onward is *Sanyasashram* for total renunciation.

Consistent with this age-old wisdom, in India tomorrow, politicians will have a strict retirement age of sixty and a term limit of eight years. The experience of retired politicians will be put to use as advisers on issues of national interest or public policy. All politicians will follow a rigorous code of ethics and will undergo a thorough background check for criminal record before running for any office. They will recognize that their job is to serve, not to rule. All this will be achieved in spite of India's chaotic democracy, remaining secular, without being a dictatorship or muzzling its free press. In tomorrow's India, the new politicians will operate like professional executives dedicated to delivering the best product and maximizing value for the citizens. What is more, the new leaders will look, act, and behave like leaders, communicating, inspiring, and radiating personality.

LEVERAGING EDUCATION

In the new India, caste-based affirmative action will be completely eliminated. The government will recognize what the experts have been saying for years that this once well-meant program is counterproductive now, it is unfair and it perpetuates the caste system and class discrimination and promotes mediocrity.

There will be adequate colleges; admissions will be strictly merit-based with no bribes or donations expected, required, offered, or accepted. In India tomorrow, education will be the great leveler. The traditional *Chaturvarnya* system of four classes will be completely eliminated. The privileged will have given way to people of merit. Young, educated, upwardly mobile Indians will advance through performance and not nepotism. While technology and IT in its present form have a rightful place in any economy, in India tomorrow, the importance of basic disciplines—physics, chemistry, mathematics, and biological sciences—will be once again recognized and fundamental research emphasized rather than every engineer of every discipline rushing to a Microsoft or SAP certification class so that he can be an "intellectual coolie" in the outsourcing business.

In addition to the core subjects of study, the education system will emphasize leadership and communication skills. Indian education system will be known for its diversity, its innovation, its excellence, and the quality of its research. India, as a member of the family of nations, will be outwardly oriented reaching out to other nations being conversant with and comfortable in their cultures while retaining its own uniqueness. The restoration and renaissance of Nalanda will be completed, and it will blossom like Harvard, MIT, Oxford, and Cambridge combined.

India tomorrow will be run by honest, fair, intelligent professional technocrats. Our seventy—and eighty-year-old politicians and "freedom fighters" will long have retired from public life, happily meditating in the Himalayas following the prescriptions of *Sanyasashram*. There will be no dynastic rule, and politics will not be a family business passing from generation to generation. The offspring of the current leaders will all have found employment commensurate with their education and capabilities.

In this dream-world of the new India, there will be no corruption anywhere. All the black money will have surfaced and found its rightful way to the national coffers. The Indian currency will be strong, convertible, respected, and accepted all over the world. There will be no unscheduled power outages anywhere. The basic necessities of life will be clean, safe, and affordable and guaranteed to all citizens. There will be public restrooms at convenient locations, and you will be able to enter them without fear and without holding your nose. Indian time will be as precise as Swiss time. Next day will mean next day and not two weeks later. Trains and planes will leave and arrive on published times. People will not spit chewed up *paan* anywhere they please.

They will stand in queues without shoving and pushing. It will be a pleasure to visit a government office. The clerk behind the desk will have learned to smile; she will be friendly, efficient, and will actually know what she is doing.

In summary, India tomorrow will be restored to its old glory. The world will recognize this and will eagerly learn from its ancient wisdom. British historian Arnold Toynbee says,

> It is already becoming clear that a chapter which had a Western beginning will have to have an Indian ending if it is not to end in the self-destruction of the human race.

A century ago, Nobel Prize winning poet, philosopher Rabindranath Tagore tried to move the nation with this wonderful vision of a heaven of freedom. Tagore's vision is quite relevant and inspiring even today.

> Where the mind is without fear
> And the head is held high;
> Where knowledge is free;
> Where the world has not been
> Broken up into fragments
> By narrow domestic walls;
> Where words come out from
> The depth of truth;
> Where tireless striving stretches its
> Arms towards perfection;
> Where the clear stream of reason
> Has not lost its way
> Into the dreary desert sand of dead habit;
> Where the mind is led forward by thee
> Into ever-widening thought and action—
> Into that heaven of freedom,
> My Father, let my country awake.

India tomorrow.

That is the tomorrow I dream of. That is the India we all long for. This is a dream. But it does not have to remain a mere fantasy.

That "tomorrow" may not come tomorrow. It may take decades. It can come, but it will come only if India, as a nation, collectively does all the right things.

Mera Bharat can be truly *Mahan. (My India can be great.)*

Will India have the will to do what it must to make it happen?

(An earlier version of this article was serialized in Voice of Asia*)*

FOUR

India and the World

SOME SOBERING STATISTICS

How does India compare with other developing countries? With almost equal populations, the Chinese economy is $10 trillion (PPP) compared to India's $4 trillion. The US, with one-fourth the population of India, has a $ 14-trillion economy. India has serious problems of child hunger and political corruption. It does not rank very high in most global surveys on parameters such as quality of life or business environment. The rankings are broad indicators of the situation at a point in time, but they do not indicate the current economic dynamism of India.

I ndia is on the move, and its young population has high ambition, great personal dreams, and aspirations as a nation. In recent years, as a member of the rapidly growing group known as BRIC (Brazil, Russia, India, and China) India has started showing up on comparison charts with the largest economies like the US and China.

However, India's presence in the top group is primarily because of its aggregate figures that are large simply because of its large population. Such numbers mean nothing to the average person on the street. Only the per capita numbers are relevant to him and would in some way be indicative of his standard of living and quality of life. In terms of per capita income and productivity numbers, India's rankings are rather low.

To be competitive and be favorably compared with the developed countries of the world, India has a long way to go. In this regard, it is interesting to see where it stands in relation to the rest of the world and particularly with its nearest rival, China. This comparison is quite relevant because of the similarities in their histories, cultures, populations, and geographic proximity.

GLOBAL GOVERNANCE

Recently, the US National Intelligence Council (NIC) and the European Union's Institute for Security Studies (EUISS) jointly issued a report entitled Global Governance 2025. The report ranks several countries based on their relative political and economic clout determined by factors such as population, GDP, defense spending, technology, etc. The report says that for 2010, the most powerful country is the US with 22 percent of the global power. This is an indicator of the relative rank in the nations of the world. Rankings for the top four nations are shown below; they indicate some decline of the West and ascent of China and India by the year 2025.

RELATIVE POLITICAL AND ECONOMIC CLOUT 2010 AND 2025

2010   USA—22%
European Union—16%
China—12%
India—8%

According to the study models, these relative strengths and positions are likely to shift as follows:

2025   USA—18%
China—16%
European Union—14%
India—10%

INCOME DISTRIBUTION IN INDIA

Despite increasing incomes, the disparity between the high and low income groups is extremely high in India. The Asian Development Bank's key indicators for Asia and Pacific 2010 report categorize the spread of Indian wealth into five groups as follows:

Income Distribution

Group	Millions of People	% Population	Income/Person/Month Rupees	Dollars
Poor	900.0	75.0	1,035 or less	23 or less
Lower mid	244.4	20.4	1,035-2,070	23-46
Mid middle	49.0	4.0	2,070-5,175	46-115
Upper mid	5.5	0.5	5,175-10,350	115-230
Rich	1.1	0.1	10,350 or more	230 or more
Total	**1,200**			

POPULATION AND GDP COMPARISON

Population and GDP figures (2011 World Bank Data) for selected countries is listed below to facilitate India's comparison with its neighbors, fellow BRIC nations, developed countries like Japan and Canada, and the economic superpowers USA and the European Union. GDP figures presented on the purchasing power parity (PPP) basis are more relevant because they take into account the varying costs of living in different countries.

India and the World: Population and GDP

	Population Millions	GDP (PPP) $ Trillions	GDP (Nominal) $ Trillions
The Big Players			
• USA	**310**	**14.5**	**14.5**
• EU	500	15.2	16.2
Other Developed			
• Japan	128	4.3	5.5
• Canada	35	1.3	1.6
BRIC			
• Brazil	190	2.2	2.1
• Russia	143	2.2	1.5
• **India**	**1,200**	**4.0**	**1.6**
• China	1,340	10.1	5.9
Neighbors			
• Pakistan	177	0.467	0.177
• Bangladesh	150	0.260	0.106
World Total	7,000	74.0	63.0

PER CAPITA GDP

The World Bank estimates per capita GDP based on purchasing power parity in the year 2010 are as follows:

Per Capita GDP based on PPP

Rank	Country	$ GDP/Capita
7	USA	47,000
25	European Union	31,000
95	China	7,500
124	India	3,500

HUNGER IN INDIA

India is sixty-seventh among eighty-four developing countries in the International Food Policy Research Institute's annual "Global Hunger Index" for 2010. Even Sudan, North Korea, and Pakistan rank higher than India. While the report shows that the proportion of undernourished in India is decreasing, it indicates that other developing countries have done better in tackling hunger. India is home to 42 percent of the underweight children below the age of five in the world. In this regard, India is on par with Bangladesh and Yemen and needs to do a much better job of planning and distribution to ensure basic food security for all of its population. This is particularly important because India is now the youngest country in the world with the most children and the largest number of people below the age of twenty-five.

ECONOMIC PARAMETERS

The tabulation below summarizes some of the important parameters of the Indian economy for the last two decades with an impressive GDP growth rate in the last several years.

Important Parameters about the Indian Economy

(Source: *Times of India*, September 22, 2010)

	1990	2007	2010
Sensex (approx.)	10,000	20,000	20,000
GDP Growth %	4.9	9.4	8.8
Forex, $ billion	1	246	284
FII Flows, $	1 m	15 b	16.4 b
FDI, $	97 m	16 b	10.7 b
Income $/Capita	390	720	970
Inflation %	9	3.4	8.5
Exchange Rs./$	17.50	39.44	45.68

- m = million, b = billion
- Sensex High—21,078 (Jan 2008); Low—8,701 (Oct 2008)

Dan Mayur

- FII—Foreign Institutional Investment
- FDI—Foreign Direct Investment

While India has quite a bit of catching up to do with its competitors in its per capita income and GDP, this tabulation does show its economic environment and its dynamism today. The major stumbling block in its potential growth is the entrenched corruption in its business and political culture.

CORRUPTION IN INDIA

Despite its present economic dynamism and future potential, Indian business environment happens to be one of the most corrupt in the world. *Bangalore Mirror* (September 9, 2010) reported that according to Mr. Pratyush Sinha, retired vigilance commissioner of India, one in three Indians is utterly corrupt. *Transparency International* puts India as eighty-seventh on its Corruption Perception Index of 178 countries surveyed in 2010. Denmark, Singapore, and New Zealand are the least corrupt with a score of 9.3 out of a max of 10. India is at 3.3, and Somalia is last at 1.1. Scandinavia, Western European countries, and North America are way ahead of India, and even China, at number 78, seems to be less corrupt than India. Here is a tabulation showing a few selected countries. In the table below, low score and high rank indicate a highly corrupt environment as in Somalia; a high score and low rank mean a clean environment, as in Denmark.

Corruption Perception Index 2010

Rank	Country	Score
1	Denmark	9.3
1	New Zealand	9.3
1	Singapore	9.3
6	Canada	8.9
17	Japan	7.8
22	USA	7.1
69	Brazil	3.7
78	China	3.5
87	India	3.3

134	Bangladesh	2.4
143	Pakistan	2.3
154	Russia	2.1
178	Somalia	1.1

Score scale: 10 (very clean), 0 (highly corrupt)

GLOBAL PROSPERITY RANKING

The Legatum Prosperity Index is a global assessment of wealth and well-being. It uses a holistic definition of prosperity, which includes factors ranging from economic growth to health and education, to personal freedom and governance. It presents a broad view of wealth, happiness, and prospects of the world's nations. The idea behind the index is that material wealth alone does not make for a happy society, but happy citizens are produced as much by democracy, freedom, social cohesion, and entrepreneurial opportunity.

Compiled by the London-based Legatum Institute, the Prosperity Index is based on eighty-nine variables, grouped into eight sub-indices, and claims to comprehensively rank the level of prosperity in 110 nations of the world. It is done by taking into account both economic growth and citizens' quality of life, drawing on data from various sources, including the Gallup World Poll and several other sources like the United Nations Development report. The 2010 Legatum report says that India's low ranking is due to its poor health care, failing to prevent systemic diseases or malnourishment, its weak infrastructure, a poor education system, and low levels of social capital.

Global Prosperity Ranking

Rank	Country
1	**Norway**
2	**Denmark**
3	Australia
4	New Zealand
5	**Sweden**
6	Canada

7	**Finland**
8	Switzerland
9	The Netherlands
10	**USA**
52	China
91	**India**
107	Pakistan
109	Zimbabwe

LIVABILITY RANKING

In August 2010, *Newsweek* conducted a survey of nations of the world with the following question:

> "If you were born today, which country would provide you the very best opportunity to live a healthy, safe, reasonably prosperous and upwardly mobile life?"

The survey considered factors like economic dynamism, education, health, quality of life, etc. The rankings based on this survey are listed in the following tabulation.

Overall Ranking of Livability in the Country

1	**Finland**	21	Spain	41	Panama	61	Kazakhstan	81	Vietnam
2	Switzerland	22	Israel	42	Peru	62	Colombia	82	S. Africa
3	**Sweden**	23	Italy	43	UAE	63	Philippines	83	Syria
4	Australia	24	Slovenia	44	Uruguay	64	S. Arabia	84	Guatemala
5	Luxembourg	25	CzechRep	45	Mexico	65	Tunisia	85	Algeria
6	**Norway**	26	Greece	46	Argentina	66	SriLanka	86	Ghana
7	**Canada**	27	Portugal	47	Jamaica	67	Morocco	87	Kenya
8	Netherlands	28	Croatia	**48**	**Brazil**	68	Paraguay	**88**	**Bangladesh**
9	**Japan**	29	Poland	49	Ukraine	69	Azerbaijan	**89**	**Pakistan**
10	**Denmark**	30	Chile	50	Cuba	70	Ecuador	90	Madagascar
11	**USA**	31	Slovakia	**51**	**Russia**	71	Venezuela	91	Senegal
12	Germany	32	Estonia	52	Turkey	72	ElSalvador	92	Yemen
13	NewZealand	33	Hungary	53	Jordan	73	Indonesia	93	Tanzania

14	UK	34	Lithuania	54	Qatar	74	Egypt	94	Ethiopia
15	S. Korea	35	CostaRica	55	Dom Rep	75	Nicaragua	95	Mozambique
16	France	36	Latvia	56	Belarus	76	Honduras	96	Uganda
17	Ireland	37	Malaysia	57	Albania	77	Bolivia	97	Zambia
18	Austria	38	Bulgaria	58	Thailand	**78**	**India**	98	Cameroon
19	Belgium	39	Romania	**59**	**China**	79	Iran	99	Nigeria
20	Singapore	40	Kuwait	60	Oman	80	Botswana	100	Burkina Faso

In terms of overall livability, India ranks seventy-eight in a group of one hundred nations.

INDIA AND CHINA

Until the early nineteenth century, China and India controlled half of the world's economy. Today, China and India are poised to regain that status in the foreseeable future. China, with a 2010 GDP of almost $6 trillion (nominal), recently passed Japan as the world's second largest economy.

While China's economic growth comes mostly from exports, India's comes primarily from domestic consumption. China's domestic consumption is a mere 35 percent of its GDP. In contrast, India's domestic consumption is about 70 percent of its GDP, comparable to the US. That is why India weathered the world economic meltdown of 2008 better than most countries. In recent years, its economy is growing at almost thrice the rate of the US. In the past twenty years, India has doubled its per capita income every ten years. But how does it compare with China, its neighbor and the nearest rival?

Growth in China is attributable to its surging construction boom and exports. Its investment spending is approaching 50 percent of GDP. India's growth is attributable mainly to domestic consumption and construction. China's construction activity and price inflation are approaching "bubble" levels because of speculation. That, plus its rapid growth of credit through essentially unregulated banking and excessive dependence on exports make the Chinese economy more risky than India's.

India will enjoy a significant advantage in the size and age of its workforce in the coming years. It is reaping a "demographic dividend" in a sense since half of its 1.2 billion people are under the age of twenty-five. In the next ten years, it will add some 80 to 110 million new workers. In contrast, China's population is aging, and India is projected to overtake China in the next ten years.

India is the world's largest democracy. Its entrepreneurial drive comes from the private sector, not from its state-owned enterprises. So far, the Indian economy has not been driven by exports. Its trade with the US, around$60 billion a year, is comparatively small. So is its trade with China, about $50 billion a year. These trade figures are growing as India puts more resources into its manufacturing sector to revamp and expand it. The problems and opportunities in India, from a foreign perspective, are summarized below.

India: Problems

- Widespread poverty, infant mortality, and malnutrition
- Discrimination against women and untouchables in certain segments of the society
- Endemic corruption
- Dynastic politics, slow-moving government with a large bureaucracy
- Environmental degradation—deforestation, dried riverbeds, and depleting water tables
- Inadequate infrastructure—roads, power, water and waste disposal
- Security issues due to continued insurgency in Kashmir and a Maoist rebellion called the Naxalite movement, in addition to sporadic occurrences of Islamic terrorism

India: Strengths and Opportunities

- A stable democracy
- Entrepreneurial spirit and the world's youngest population
- A $500 billion infrastructure program with opportunities in clean energy technologies and construction of roads, railways, and subways
- Service opportunities to cater to the needs of an aspiring middle class of three hundred million and growing
- G20 membership with free trade deals with countries like Singapore, S. Korea, and the Association of Southeast Asian Nations (ASEAN), and strong trading relationships with other countries in the region

The representative tabulations presented earlier in this essay are indicative of the problems facing India as well as the opportunities available in its growing economy. Some of the figures, especially the rankings in various categories can be depressing. But it must be remembered that the data and the rankings are developed by organizations in the West looking at India through Western eyes using their criteria, and therefore, a certain degree of subjectivity is inevitable. Besides, these numbers are continuously changing from year to year or even quarter to quarter.

It is noteworthy that all Scandinavian countries are in the top ten no matter what the ranking is for—clean business environment (low corruption), prosperity, or overall livability. The USA is typically immediately below Scandinavia, and India generally finds itself in the third or fourth quartile.

While such figures are broad indicators of the situation at a point in time, they fail to capture the current economic dynamism of India and the renewed spirit of entrepreneurship and drive of a new generation of its young businessmen. Certainly, India has a long way to go to be where it wants to be, but such low rankings, rather than being depressing, should provide a direction and serve as guides and motivators for its growth and progress.

FIVE

Bangalore Diary

Bangalore is India's Silicon Valley. It is a magnet for domestic and foreign high technology companies and is the fastest growing city in India. However, Bangalore inside the gated walls of its fabulous residential communities and its numerous high-tech parks and the common man's Bangalore outside these walls are two completely different worlds. Outside the compounds, Bangalore looks like any other town in India.

India is changing, and one of the most dramatic and welcome examples of this a visitor to Bangalore sees is its new international airport with world-class decor, excellent facilities for travelers, and immaculate maintenance. This is the first noticeable major change. With hassle-free immigration and customs procedures, courteous staff and easy baggage handling, arrival at the airport is smooth-sailing. There are direct flights from Europe to Bangalore, Hyderabad and Pune, avoiding the traditional points of entry like Mumbai and Delhi; and this is quite a convenience for US and European travelers. Dealing with things outside the airport, of course, requires an exercise in expectation management. For people like me, arriving from the clean and cool environment of Scandinavia and the quiet, comfortable, and peaceful life there, the colorful, cacophonous chaos of India takes a significant mental and physical adjustment.

CONSUMERISM

The second most impressive change as discussed earlier in the essay entitled "India Today" is the advent of unabashed, US-style consumerism in its major cities. Shops of all shapes and sizes, from the old-fashioned mom-and-pop boutiques to megamalls are ubiquitous teeming with American and European brand-name products. Shopping at Bangalore's Hypermarket is a particularly enjoyable experience. It is loaded with an impressive array of familiar but highly unexpected products like Del Monte prunes, Lindt chocolates, and Silk soymilk just to name a few; and of course, there is an abundance of local fare. Most of the Indian-manufactured products are of high quality, nicely packaged, and easily affordable.

In terms of creature comforts, be it the latest electronic gadgets or the finest liquors, there is really nothing that is not available in a place like Bangalore. The days of the uncles and aunts from "phoren lands" coming home with huge bags loaded with gifts and goods are gone. They now take back with them the better and much cheaper Indian products of all kinds. This is a dramatic change in a span of a relatively few years.

India's middle class, about three hundred million people by most accounts, appears to have gone on a shopping rampage, many with borrowed money, and this seems to be adequate to sustain India's consumption growth. This is amply visible in a vibrant city like Bangalore, teeming with two-paycheck families of young urban professionals. Further, looking at the large size of the remaining population, about nine hundred million people, the consumer market here has an unlimited growth potential for decades to come. This augurs well for India especially in the light of the fact that much of the developed West is saturated, stagnating, or even declining.

HOUSING CONSTRUCTION

Concurrent with consumerism in India is the explosion of construction activity in the Industrial, commercial, and residential arena. This is evident all over the country, from Kolkata to Kozhikode to Bhivandi. But Bangalore is the epicenter of this mammoth effort where apartment towers, office buildings, and IT parks are mushrooming up in a frenzy of construction activity not seen outside of Shanghai of the last two decades. Some of the construction is quite good and elegant, some shoddy and outright ugly but much of it, what seems like, without a broader master plan or adequate infrastructure for roads and utilities. Heavy construction equipment, cranes, scaffoldings, and piles of construction material—pipes, bricks, sand, steel beams, and dirt and stones from dug-up trenches and broken sidewalks are visible all over Bangalore.

SECURITY AND UNIFORMS

A very noticeable fact these days is the appearance of highly enhanced security at most places in the current environment of rapid growth and prevailing concerns for terrorism. This is quite evident in Bangalore because of its many gated communities and high-tech, high-security areas. There are teams of uniformed security guards, mostly emaciated skinny youth in ill-fitting garb, at offices, apartment complexes, malls, and assorted public places flashing badges, stopping vehicles, checking bags, purses, and trunks of vehicles, writing down names and numbers and making verification calls. And yet one quickly senses their lackadaisical style and porosity of the system. Generally, they are very friendly people but guards, they just are not.

The most hilarious and incongruent part is their lanky posture, tentative facial expression, spineless body language, and willingness to grant concessions to entering cars or individuals at the entrance in return for a kind or flattering word, without any thoughtful discretion whatsoever. Alternatively, one can appear important, slightly raise his voice, and make a rushed entry into the building. The more important you look, the easier is the entry. The guards normally operate in groups of three or four, congregating in a huddle to share a smoke or exchange gossip or for intently perusing over the log books of incoming and outgoing cars. These poor guards are the exact opposites of the image they are expected to convey.

Think of the beefy, burly, smartly-dressed, awe-inspiring security guards or policemen that one encounters in the West. But never mind. Surely, this new Indian security system provides a lot of employment. The primary function of the guards is to salute the babu's coming and going. In the six months of my stay in Bangalore, I have been saluted more times than in my forty years in the US. I must admit it feels good. Here in India, we genuinely love salutes, garlands, rubber stamps, signatures, and approvals—anything that makes you feel important will do.

HIGH-TECH INDIA

There is no doubt that the IT and high-tech businesses together with the explosion of cell phone and computer usage have propelled segments of Indian population to leapfrog into the twenty-first century. Bangalore, the job-robbing capital of the world according to the laid-off, ailing masses of the developed countries, is truly California's Silicon Valley and Boston's famed Route 128 all rolled into one for India. With other centers like Gurgaon and Noida and Pune and Hyderabad also attracting large number of foreign and domestic entrepreneurs, it is with much pride that Indians have started referring to the country as "High-tech India" as opposed to "Agrarian India." But such characterization is a little premature because the progress is extremely spotty, uneven, and perhaps with questionable priorities.

The well-known contrasts of India attain a spectacular level in a high-tech place like Bangalore because of its IT-driven pockets of wealth. The sight of iPod-totting eight-year-olds running around naked on a narrow strip between their slum and a luxury high-rise haughtily promoting itself "the Belgravia—three BHK (bath, hall, and kitchen) starting from Rs. 4 crores (one crore equals ten million)" is not uncommon and is a very apt, amusing but sad reminder of the current situation. But Belgravia? (Belgravia is one of the most exclusive neighborhoods in the most expensive part of London). I thought India kicked the British out sixty years ago. And did it not banish the Anglicized names, the Bombays and Calcuttas, with much fanfare and replaced them with Mumbais and Kolkatas more palatable to the masses? Apparently, eliminating British names has been the major, and frequently the only, contribution of elected governments for uplifting the lives of the citizens. So why are all these Hyde Parks and Belgravias and Dorchesters cropping up in cities like Bangalore? A fine resort place in Coorg, Karnataka, I visited recently is called, of all things, Orange County, as in Los Angeles!

R AND D IN BANGALORE

The subject of R and D in India, both in industry and in the academia, attracts considerable interest. The quality of technical talent available in India and especially in places like Bangalore is quite high. This is for two reasons. First, the high caliber of the students graduating from the nation's premier institutions like the IITs, and second, the continually growing stream of experienced NRIs returning to India and particularly to Bangalore. Recognizing this, multinational companies are expanding both the funding and the scope of their operations here beyond routine production work into R and D. Expatriate managers arriving in India specifically to set up R and D facilities report that the quality of R and D here is quite high and is improving rapidly. They are impressed by the people they are hiring. Their satisfaction with Indian researchers and the economic imperatives are such that some of their high-cost facilities in the US and Europe are being closed down or relocated as places like Bangalore expand.

TWO BANGALORES

There is no better example than Bangalore to illustrate the point that there are many Indias within India. The Bangalore inside the gated walls of its fabulous residential communities and its numerous high-tech parks and the Bangalore outside these walls are two completely different worlds. The gated residential communities have million-dollar, single-family homes reminiscent of any affluent suburb in the US. And most of the IT parks are self-sufficient mini-cities with beautifully designed and maintained shining glass buildings, gorgeous landscaping with lush tropical vegetation, reliable power and water supply, some with shopping, living accommodation, and numerous other facilities like clinics, banks, and restaurants for the employees.

In other words, this is Thomas Friedman's India, the very limited little oasis that he thinks rest of India is like—a country that offers global companies, continental food, international schools, and domestic help; a clean, orderly, wealthy, high-tech place with secure, high-paying, wonderful jobs, and complete freedom from outsourcing.

Outside the campus walls, Bangalore looks like any other town in India—crowded, dusty, and dirty with puddles and potholes on the road with particularly bad sidewalks and sights, sounds, and smells that are a major assault on your senses. It is not worse or better than other Indian cities but is a major disappointment for this is very inconsistent with its hyped-up image as the economic engine of modern India. While inside the IT parks, Western-style conveniences are taken for granted, the *aam janata* (general masses) outside struggles with basic necessities what with sudden unpredictable power and water cuts, nauseating pollution, and garbage-strewn roads. Whether one likes it or not, this also illustrates what motivated, hardworking people in the private sector can accomplish in contrast with the "who cares" attitude and the general apathy and lack of accountability, vision, pride, and honesty in the public sector.

It does not have to be so. Starting with Texas Instruments' first facility in 1986, the IT industry in Bangalore is only twenty-five years old. But way before that, soon after independence, when Prime Minister Jawaharlal Nehru sought a prominent role for public sector enterprises, Bangalore was an attractive location for some of them because of the availability of cheap electrical power, educated workforce, and the presence of institutions like the Indian Institute of Science. Thus, Indian companies like HAL, BEL, ITI, and HMT came to be established in and around Bangalore. In addition, Bangalore attracted and became a major center for garment manufacturers and exporters. In their book *Bengaluru, Bangalore, Bengaluru: Imaginations and Their Times* authors Narendar Pani and Sindhu Radhakrishna provide an excellent account of Bangalore's industrial development. It just seems odd that with all these industries, an able workforce, and wealth creation possibility, Bangalore does not look significantly different from other Indian cities outside of its IT parks, of course. If there is any trickle-down effect, it is not very visible.

QUALITY OF LIFE

In a place like Bangalore, the young, college-educated men and women, especially in any kind of technical field, have plenty of job opportunities, incomes their parents never had (even after accounting for inflation), and ability to own a flat and a motorized vehicle, travel and educate their children. Two pay-check families are common within this group, and they are particularly well off with increasingly better quality of life. It is very questionable whether this is true at all for the literally millions of villagers that are leaving the rural areas, causing a very rapid and unplanned urbanization and thus straining the already weak infrastructure of most Indian cities like Bangalore. The lure of the cities is great. But there is no space, no housing, no water, power, and sanitation for them.

QUALITY OF LIFE FOR EXPATRIATES

Judging from my own brief experience and that of some expat friends in Bangalore, I can say that the expats enjoy an incredibly cushy life here, at least within the confines of their well-appointed apartments and in their modern, global office facilities. A two—or three-bedroom apartment in excellent location, fully furnished with linen and cleaning service and totally equipped American-style kitchens and toilettes can be rented for anything in the range of $2,500-$4,000 per month including all utilities. Many apartment complexes have free breakfast service, an á la carte kitchen plus they provide a dedicated butler, a part-time cook, and a domestic cleaner for each apartment. And for $1,000-$1,200 per month, you get a chauffeur-driven car from your employer. All this is in addition to appropriate overseas assignment uplifts and allowances in your compensation. Life is good.

Or is it?

You begin to wonder about all the domestic help you have but you absolutely do not need. In forty years in the US, we have never had domestic help on a daily basis, never needed it, could not afford it, and we do not know how to order around another human being to pick up after us. The whole concept made me uncomfortable. The four people assigned to help us were all young lads of twenty to twenty-two from Bihar or Orissa, all high school dropouts, each making three thousand rupees a month (or one hundred rupees a day, about two dollars), except for the driver who made twice that much. One hates to use the horrible word "servants"; unfortunately, a most noticeably distinguishing aspect of India is servants. They are everywhere. India is full of servants.

They were all bright, hardworking, honest kids thankful for the opportunity of sending little sums of fifty or sixty dollars every month back home to their impoverished parents in the village. These were kids, younger than our children, washing some fat and lazy expat's dishes when they should have been going to college, chasing girls, building foundations of life for themselves and their country. This is slavery in a different form.

On my part, I adopted Dhaneshwar, one of the helper boys, during our stay in Bangalore. One of six children from a family of destitute farmers in a little village near Bhubaneshwar in the state of Orissa, he was a ninth-grade dropout and had forgotten even the basic skills of reading and writing. A very pleasant, humble young man, he became my loyal friend and a favored student. We spent three hours every afternoon studying English and basic math. His goal was to study "komputers" and start a computer school in his village. And yet the class-consciousness is so high among India's poor that it took me two full months to get him to sit on a chair at my study desk during our lessons. He was most comfortable sitting on the floor, at my feet, where he thought he belonged. This is so sad, and yet there is hope.

I left Bangalore a while ago, but I hope Dhaneshwar is continuing his studies for komputers somewhere. But one wonders how many millions of Dhaneshwars are out there and what they are doing.

SIX

O Calcutta!

Calcutta, renamed Kolkata, was the first capital established in India by the British East India Company. Once a beautiful city, today it is a very crowded place with severe congestion and impossible traffic. The Bengalis are known for their performing arts, and Kolkata is a fun place for the art lover. The city's social life revolves around its many British era clubs, which desperately struggle to retain their decadent charm. Undoubtedly, the most enjoyable annual event in festival-loving India is the ten-day celebration of Durga Puja in Kolkata.

Calcutta, now Kolkata, one of the largest cities in the world, has been known historically as the City of Joy, the Paris of the East, and the cultural center of India—thanks to its famous sons like philosopher Swami Vivekananda, poet Rabindranath Tagore (India's first Nobel Prize winner), botanist Jagdish Chandra Bose, author Bankim Chandra, moviemaker par excellence Satyajit Ray, flute maestro Pannalal Ghosh, and firebrand freedom fighter Netaji Subhash Chandra Bose among others. In modern times, Kolkata also has the dubious distinction of having one of the largest slum areas of Asia and is among the poorest and heavily polluted cities of the world.

CALCUTTA OF THE BRITISH ERA

There is no doubt that as the first capital of British India hundred plus years ago, this must have been a truly magnificent city on par with any great metropolis of Europe. Relics of grand Victorian architecture are evident all over the place. The Writer's Building, the first office of the East India Company, occupied today by the West Bengal Government, is still recognized the world over as a superb masterpiece of English architecture. The Victoria Memorial is another wonderful, Taj Mahal-like structure. For the initiated, there is still a lot of British history to see here, including several churches and monuments of the likes of Warren Hastings, Lord Curzon, and others. Curiously, most of the original British names of places and streets—Dalhousie Square, Russell Street, Auckland Place, etc., have all been retained.

KOLKATA TODAY

But Kolkata today is no London. Unfortunately, its majestic buildings, not having seen a paintbrush or even a broom in decades of neglect by the government are in a pathetic state of dilapidation. The well-planned, tree-shaded avenues and spacious parks of years bygone are taken over by the homeless, beggars, and street hawkers. Except for a few selected places, in most areas there are garbage, cars, people, pollution, and dug-up pavements all over; but then, this is typical of most major cities in India. And just as in Mumbai, Delhi, Bangalore, Hyderabad, and Chennai, Kolkata is experiencing a heavy construction boom all over the city in recent years.

The congestion defies imagination. Kolkata has road surface to city area ratio of less than 6 percent compared to as much as 50 percent in most major cities in the world and around 15 percent in India. With an impossibly high population density of around ninety thousand per square kilometer, this is a beehive of human beings. In this city, some fifteen million people live, breathe, urinate in public places, or otherwise pollute, commute in decrepit buses packed like sardines. And then there are daily reports of crumbling buildings. The whole infrastructure of the city—roads and transportation, housing, water and power supply—is inadequate and overstressed; and the situation is getting worse because of the new construction. During the monsoon season, June through September, it rains frequently, flooding the streets, further paralyzing the city.

And yet all is not bad. Amidst the cacophony of this crazy urban jungle, on the banks of the mighty river Hoogley is a place of divine serenity, extraordinary cleanliness, and peace—Vivekananda's Belur Math, run by the Ramakrishna Mission. This beautiful shrine takes you completely out of the busy bustling city. It is hard to believe that this is a part of Kolkata. It is a must visit for any spiritually minded visitor.

The Hoogley, an offshoot of the Ganges, is a very impressive river here. The Howrah Bridge (now Rabindra Setu) associated with Kolkata as intimately as the Big Ben is with London or the Statue of Liberty is with New York is as impressive as the river on which it is built.

THE CLUB CULTURE

Kolkata's social life revolves around its many exclusive clubs more than in any other city in India including Delhi and Mumbai. The rich and famous of Kolkata hang out at these relics of the British era, and much of the entertaining happens at these clubs rather than at private residences. The Tollygunge Club, the Royal Turf Club, the Bengal Club, the Saturday Club, and the Royal Golf Club, reputed to be the second oldest golf club in the world, are some of the watering holes popular with the local glitterati. Amidst the abysmal poverty, these clubs are another world representing oases of obscene wealth where conspicuous consumption is the order of the day. Desperately emulating anything Western, the wealthy patrons of these clubs are still clinging to the trappings of the good life of the sahibs of the British Raj. In this regard, Kolkata seems to be quite different from other Indian cities. Most of these club facilities are over a hundred years old with the same architecture, same decor and furniture, same *sepoys* (peons), and same traditions that existed then.

At the country clubs, potbellied businessmen and corporate executives trod on magnificently verdant golf courses, frequently in uncoordinated golf gear, followed by an entourage of caddies who toil for hours to get *baksheesh* of a pittance at the end of the day. Some of the ancient club-houses still retain their original charm. While the men putter around, plump, wealthy wives gossip over imported drinks and mutton samosas. The whole thing is so anachronistic, so out of place and so immensely enjoyable.

THE BENGALI PEOPLE

The Bengalis are a friendly lot, and despite the aggravation of the congestion, traffic and pollution there, I have very fond memories of Kolkata, its wonderful people, and their mouthwatering cuisine.

But even before you get to know the Bengalis, you fall in love with "*amaar shonar Bongla*" (our golden Bengal), the land itself. Flying into Kolkata, looking down from the plane window just before landing, you are absolutely stunned by the lush, verdant land below. Everything is naturally irrigated emerald green, beautiful little patches of farmland dotted with coconut trees, quaint little huts with thatched roofs, and waterlogged paddies and not an inch of brown earth visible anywhere. The Ganges delta is one of the most fertile, and that, coupled with the monsoons, keeps the area evergreen. Compared to the dry, arid lands of Maharashtra and most of central India, this explosion of various shades of green makes quite an impression on the first-time visitor.

On the cultural landscape too, Kolkata is at the forefront. The Bengalis are a very talented and artistic people known for their music, painting, literature, theater, and moviemaking. Eminent music teacher and critic Sapna Devi observes, "*In each Bengali household, there is art-learning and patronage of some kind of art.*" Rabindra-sangeet and Tagore's plays are among the most popular entertainment/art forms here. And undoubtedly, one of the major gifts to the nation from Bengal in the area of the performing arts is the remarkable Shankar family led by the incomparable, internationally famous sitar maestro Pandit Ravi Shankar and the renowned dancing members of his family—Sachin and Uday Shankar. And then there are so many others from this region in the field of Indian classical music.

Kolkata is also a shopping paradise for women of discriminating taste. Bengali cotton textiles—especially Calcutta saris—are among the most popular items for their beautiful designs, colors, and fabric quality.

Bengalis are hearty eaters and are known for their delicious seafood and rice dishes. My favorite is the delectable *maccher-zol*, a spicy fish curry. That is simply out of this world with plain rice. But the Bengalis are most famous for and most fond of their sweets—*mishti doi, roshagolla, chomchom, and shondesh*—all dairy-based sugary preparations. Not just the Bengalis but Indians all over the country love desserts made of sugar and milk in one form or another, possibly replicating the taste of the very popular Hindu god, Lord Krishna, who was known to devour heaps of cheese, yogurt, and butter as a child. There is no known record of his lipid profile and cholesterol levels, but I wonder about all that plaque buildup in the divine arteries at a young age.

On a lighter note, my Bengali friends jokingly told me that Bengali men, in general, are known to be the classic, lazy non-doers. Given a choice, they would sit back, chillax (chill and relax), and enjoy life, reading a book or listening to music. Bengali women are the doers and run the household with a firm hand. The first job of a new daughter-in-law in a Bengali home is to separate and wean the boy, now her husband, from his doting mother.

DURGA PUJA

The most memorable part of my Kolkata experience is its world-famous annual celebration of the Durga Puja, the biggest and the most important festival in Bengal. Many Bengali films, albums, and books are released to coincide with this festival. The state government declares special holidays for the festivities. Gatherings of friends called *Aadda* in Bengali are common in many homes and restaurants. Commercially this sociocultural event is as big as Christmas in the Western world or Diwali in other parts of India or the Carnival in Rio de Janeiro. It is also a time to display the extraordinary talent and organization skills of the local people in creating artistic, gigantic images of the goddess Durga and magnificent decorations in specially created football-field-size tents called *pandals*.

Visiting *pandals* with friends and family, socializing and sampling the food from stalls around them is known as *pandal-hopping*. It seems the entire population of fifteen million people of Kolkata is out every night for ten days participating and enjoying a nonstop citywide party.

In Kolkata alone, more than two thousand *pandals* are set up, each ornately decorated, vying for attention, inviting people and trying to outdo the *pandal* next door. The entire city is adorned with colorful lights. People from all over the country visit the city at this time, and every night is one mad carnival of *pandal*-hopping and eating out. The already heavy traffic comes to an absolute standstill, and walking is the only option. But people love it.

The scale and grandeur of the celebration boggles the mind. The enormous effort, the energy, and the resources expended in these events, be it Durga Puja in Bengal or Ganesh Utsav in Maharashtra, make you wonder about the alternative possibilities of their use in a poor country like India. But then that is for the bean counters to worry about. These festivals serve an important social need. They bring people together, break the monotony of a routine and difficult life, and provide an outlet for people's talent and creativity.

SEVEN

Lalbagcha Raja and the CWG

Religious festivals are big in India and play an important role in the lives of the people. In addition to their spiritual significance, festivals satisfy a social need that cannot be met by any government programs or technological innovations. Many festivals are celebrated communally through large volunteer organizations. Their seamless operation can put many government bureaucracies to shame.

Undoubtedly, one of the unique joys of being in India is to observe, from a distance, the incredible extravaganza and the colorful pageantry of traditional celebrations of cherished religious festivals like the *Ramlila* and *Holi* in north India, *Janmashtami,* and *Ganesh Utsav* in Maharashtra, and the spectacular *Durga Puja* in west Bengal among others. Indians are by nature very festive and social people. Each region has its unique festivals and the locals celebrate them with great gusto and fanfare.

In recent years, a lot of these celebrations have gone high-tech true to the image of the modern IT India. There is nothing surprising about the faith and devotion of the masses and their unparalleled enthusiasm about the rituals and the music and the dancing and the processions. But what is so impressive is the ever-increasing amount of material wealth and human effort pouring into these events, the use of technology, the art and creativity manifested in the spectacular decorations, and above all, the impeccable organization and project management of these gigantic events planned and executed mainly by volunteers in large and small private entities.

GANESH FESTIVAL

The scale of operation and the mass of humanity involved in the whole enterprise is most impressive. *Bappa Ganesh* (Lord Ganesh) celebration is popular all over India, but its importance in Maharasthra, and particularly in Mumbai and Pune, is several cuts above the rest of the country. It must be so because so many of the local politicians, business tycoons, cricket stars, and Bollywood celebrities are seen falling over each other to be photographed paying their homage to Bappa in the most popular locations. Actually the locations become more popular after they have done so. Thankfully, these places of worship are packed wall-to-wall, leaving no room for our filmy heroes and heroines to burst out into their pelvis-thrusting, rear-end wiggling dance and song routines in front of the Bappa. Good sense prevails.

In Mumbai, out of literally thousands of formally installed idols, the biggest in size as well as importance is the image of Ganapati in the Lalbag area, popularly called *Lalbagcha Raja* or simply, Raja. (Lalbagcha means "of Lalbag" in Marathi, the local language.)

I happened to be in India during these festivities in the year 2010. As always, the size of the procession and the flawless execution of *"visarjan"* (immersion concluding the ten-day celebration) festivities of the Raja were both beautifully orchestrated and grand in scale, but the thing that was most noteworthy was the fact that during the procession, the Raja stopped at a mosque along the way to accept puja and prayers from Muslim members of the community. This was a beautiful and gratifying gesture of harmony as the nation anxiously awaited court decision on the Ayodhya / Babri Masjid, a flash point in the on-going Hindu/Muslim rift in India.

Just like Lalbag in Mumbai, another most spectacular procession is that of the famous *Dagdoo Halwai Ganapati* in the sister city of Pune. The artistry, the decorations, and the money involved are beyond imagination; and it is hard to believe that this spectacle is in India and not in some wealthiest of wealthy dreamlands. The decorations are exceedingly rich and ornate, making the overall ambience simply marvelous. The enthusiasm of the masses, their devotion, and the festive spirit, not to mention the amazing talent and artistry of the volunteers and participating high school band troupes, remind one of the extravaganza of the Tournament of Roses Parade, the Mardi Gras in New Orleans, and the Carnival in Rio all combined, sans the sex, of course.

THE VALUE OF FESTIVALS

Celebrations like these have considerable value in bringing the community together and providing a forum for the performing arts and an outlet for creativity. Human beings need something to put their faith into, something to kindle the hope in the hearts and some object of worship to thank for the success and the good fortune that might come their way. And these festivals are great levelers. The rich and the poor, the masters and the servants, all get the same "*darshana*" (sighting) and eat the same "*prasada*" (holy food distributed as a blessing of the Lord). Religious festivals sustain societies and cultures in a way that governments cannot.

FIASCO OF THE COMMONWEALTH GAMES

Contrast this Ganesh Festival celebration with the fiasco that was unfolding in New Delhi, the nation's capital on a daily basis regarding the Commonwealth Games (CWG) in the autumn of 2010. One of the goals of these games was to announce India's arrival on the international scene as a legitimate global player. In many ways, the ten-day Ganesh Utsav in

Mumbai and the two-week long CWG in New Delhi were similar in terms of the number of people involved and the joy these events might bring to them. But there were important differences. The CWG entailed a lot of international hoopla, heavy government involvement, need for new infrastructure, and an absurd amount of taxpayer money with inherent opportunities for corruption.

In comparison, celebrations like Ganesh Utsav are activities wholeheartedly and spontaneously performed by private volunteer groups without the need for any special infrastructure and no inclination or opportunity for corruption. The sad thing is that what Mumbai can do for *Ganesh Utsav* or what Kolkata can do for *Durga Puja,* New Delhi could not do for the CWG as evidenced by the following, just a week before the start of the games:

- The September 23, 2010, *Times of India* front-page headline
  "More Shame Heaped on CWG—chunks of ceiling fall at main venue"

- The September 22, 2010, *Times of India* front-page headline
  "Games Become India's Shame—Bridge to main stadium crashes"

In the same issue of *TOI*, some of the participant nations said,

> Scotland: *"There are stray dogs on beds; shit in rooms"*
> England: *"Toilets disgusting; electrical equipment unsafe"*
> Canada: *"Towers full of rubbish; conditions unacceptable"*
> New Zealand: *"No faith things will change"*

The CWG organizing committee secretary general Shri Lalit Bhanotji said,

> *"It is not such a big issue which we should be ashamed of. . . . Westerners have different standards of hygiene, we have different standards."*

One cannot find a better example of denial and premature declaration of victory in the entire human history. Accidents do happen, and while the incessant barrage of headlines like these is depressing to any lover of India, the real shame is in the arrogance, indifference, and insensitivity displayed in the secretary general's ludicrous remarks. India has different standards of hygiene!

CWG BUDGET ESTIMATE

Authors Boria Majumdar and Nalin Mehta claim in their book *Sellotape Legacy: Delhi and the Commonwealth Games* that the original budget estimate of India's showpiece CWG was Rs. 617 crores in 2002. It escalated to a figure 114 times larger at Rs. 70 thousand crores; that is eleven zeroes after seven or Rs. 700000000000. Maybe the Indian pride demanded that this be its answer to China's extravaganza for the 2008 Beijing Olympics. But then think of the schools and hospitals and roads India needs. A recent study by the University of Oxford measured levels of education, health, and living standard in the world's poorest countries. This study also shows that India continues to be predominantly poor. In fact, there are more poor people in eight Indian states than in the twenty-six poorest African countries combined. This CWG bonanza may be indicative of India's misplaced priorities. Here is an interesting mental acrobatic. The CWG budget amounted to seven hundred rupees for every one of our one billion people. Alternatively, if 1 percent of our population is considered super poor, like the unfortunate beggars, for those ten million people, this expenditure amounts to an incredible seventy thousand rupees per person. If such money is spent on education, India can take a big bite out of its perennial poverty.

THE LESSONS

Two things come out of this, loud and clear:

First, India, as a country, has made a lot of progress; and its people should be rightly proud of what has been accomplished in the past twenty years. But it has a very long way to go to attain international stature in most things other than IT.

I think holding events like the CWG (I am hearing rumblings about bidding for the 2020 Olympics!) represent misplaced priorities and the Rs.70,000 crore price tag is simply unconscionable. While there is a desperate urge to be recognized internationally in a big hurry as a nation, India is just not ready yet. There is a school of thought that says progress must be made on all fronts simultaneously. That may be true after a minimum level of development and standard of living are attained. Until then, you must have thoughtful, clear, and inviolable priorities that focus on the basics. Expensive events like the CWG cannot be such a priority.

Before we worry about beautiful residences for the CWG athletes, we need basic sanitation and drinking water for our masses. Before we worry about the falling bridges at the CWG venues, we need pothole-free roads in our cities. It takes a certain culture and a degree of well-being for the entire country before you can bring about a successful international event even in a single city like New Delhi.

Hillary Clinton says to educate one child properly, "*it takes a village*," meaning help is needed from every quarter. Likewise, the dedication of the entire country is needed for holding something like the CWG. For national success, you must have a special national psychology that comes only from general well-being and a sense of pride and purpose, all so painfully absent in the organizing committee secretary general's comment.

The second conclusion one can draw from this sordid happening in New Delhi is about the absence of learning at the national level. Just as human beings learn new things and remember, store, and recall what they have learned, families, communities, and nations are also learning entities. The learning at the group level is through experiences, projects executed, wars, natural calamities, and successes and failures in handling them. Indians are great at learning and transferring the learned knowledge at the individual and family levels. A politician's son easily becomes a politician, and a movie star's children routinely become movie stars. Such natural learning is easy within families. But it is both slow and difficult in the context of larger groups like whole nations, especially in the absence of stepwise, systematic development.

What the GaneshUtsava groups have learned collectively over a century of celebrations, India, as a nation, has not had a chance to learn, store, recall, and use. There are no shortcuts. This is a matter of national will, time, and experience; and until that happens, India will be better off focusing on the basics—providing sanitation, water, power, and education to the 75 percent of its population categorized as poor. Successful or not, the CWG could not have and did not do anything to improve the global image of India or the lives of its masses.

EIGHT

To be a Woman in India

Women could be a pampered princess or a wretched slave in India. Because of enormous diversity, there is no simple answer to the question of what it means to be a woman in India. It depends on numerous factors such as age, education, family background, marital status, and financial situation. Yet some broad generalization is possible. Educated and young professional women in the urban areas enjoy a lifestyle on par with that in the developed countries. However, in rural areas, women's lives are suppressed by superstition, religious dogma, and family tradition.

I t is indeed both presumptuous and quixotic for any man to even think of reading the female mind and attempting to write an article on a subject as complex as what it means to be a woman, be it in India or anywhere else. It is especially hard for somebody like me who has extreme difficulty in understanding his own wife's yeses, nos, and maybes, which could mean maybe, yes, and no respectively, depending upon the time, place, subject, and mood. So this effort on my part is beyond reckless. But then I find myself surrounded by high-achieving professional women of Indian origin—an eminent attorney for a daughter, a world-class software expert spouse, a banking executive sister-in-law, a poet mother, and friends who are reputed dentists, engineers, architects, authors, and physicians. And that somehow seems to qualify me.

VISION OF THE SAGES

India is a land recognized for the wisdom of its ancient sages and scriptures. Fundamental to any civilization is the family dynamic and the relationship between man and woman in the society. The woman's role in this relationship is of paramount importance. A loving woman binds the family together, sustains it, nurtures it, and makes it grow. The position and the respect the woman commands in the society is a metric of its development and sophistication. Happily, the Indian scriptures hold the woman in high esteem and prescribe attributes of an ideal woman as defined by the following seven Sanskrit words:

1. *Kirti*—That is fame or reputation she brings to her family by her work, talents, and behavior.
2. *Laxmi*—This is the wealth, material as well as spiritual, that a woman contributes.
3. *Wani*—This refers to a woman's natural sweetness, her gentle language, and the support and understanding she provides.
4. *Smriti*—This indicates a superior memory, recall, storage of knowledge, and values.
5. *Medha*—This is the woman's attribute of intelligence, sanity, logic.
6. *Dhriti*—Means courage, poise, composure.
7. *Kshama*—Signifies forgiveness, generosity, open-mindedness.

These qualities expected in women clearly indicate how they were to be viewed in the society and what was thought of them. The Hindu goddesses are implied role models for ordinary women and attest to this high expectation.

Goddess Durga is a strong woman, destroyer of evil. Goddess Saraswati is known for her intellect and knowledge. Goddess Laxmi presides over wealth and so on. In Indian mythology, the great epics *Ramayana* and *Mahabharata* portray the personalities of strong, principled, and accomplished women like *Seeta, Gandhari, Kunti,* and *Draupadi.* And this was not just in the mythology. Historically, too, women have played a significant role in Indian life—and the names of Ranee Chanamma, Ranee Laxmibai, and Jeejabai easily come to mind.

GENERAL SITUATION TODAY

Today, the actual situation of women in India is nowhere close to the prescriptions or the vision of the scriptures. At best, it is a mixed bag. The question "What does it mean to be a woman in India today?" does not lend itself to a single easy answer. India is not homogeneous Sweden where every woman (well, almost every woman) is blond, tall, slim, educated, gainfully employed, probably divorced, and independent.

What it means to be a woman in India depends on numerous factors like age, education, geographic region, family background, joint or nuclear family, religion, marital status, financial situation, urban or rural environment, and so on. Anjali Mathur, an eminent professional consultant to major business houses in India puts it cogently, *"Depending upon these factors, a woman can be a pampered princess or a wretched slave in India."*

However, notwithstanding these two extremes, some broad generalizations can still be made about what it means to be a woman in India, with certain caveats, of course.

First and foremost, it is important to know that the Indira and Sonia Gandhi's, beneficiaries of the unique dynasty-worshipping culture of Indian politics, do not represent Indian women in any shape or form. It would be foolish to rejoice over any claims that women have made phenomenal progress in India based on the status of the Gandhi women.

Today, in the twenty-first century, there are communities in parts of the country where the birth of a female child is frowned upon, frequently with very sad consequences for the mother and the child. On the other hand, in the educated middle-class families in metropolitan areas like Mumbai and Delhi, girls enjoy equal status and opportunities for education and employment and essentially the same freedoms that their counterparts in other developed countries do, although, thankfully, premarital sex is less common. In contrast, in underdeveloped rural India where educational and health-care facilities are highly inadequate, poverty and superstition still govern the ways of life. Here, females are clearly second-class citizens.

Needless to say, there are region-specific differences. With the risk inherent in broad generalizations, one can say that women from the north—mainly Punjab and Delhi area—are more outgoing and progressive than others while those from the south tend to be more conservative, old-fashioned, and religious but more focused on education. However, regardless of any qualifiers, Indian women, in general, are devoted to their families—pious, caring, and respectful of the elderly, hardworking, willing, and ready to make personal sacrifices and serve. Indian mothers are compulsive feeders of their children, whether they are six or sixty years old, and their greatest joy in life seems to be to see the children well-fed, plump, and fattened.

HISTORICAL PERSPECTIVE

Historically, age-old traditions based on the teachings of the scriptures clearly defined the male/female roles in Indian society. In general, Indians have always strongly believed in the marriage system and frowned upon divorces. Living arrangements almost always involved joint families. As in most other countries, the man was the classic "provider" to his woman and the family they created together. The woman took care of the children and the house. He worked outside, she inside. While this split of work seemed equitable, it did put some extra burden on the women in the traditional joint families where three generations coexisted and considerable adjustment was required with personal sacrifice, endurance, understanding, and compassion. Even though the division of labor was even, the man was always the dominant member of the family and the society. There is nothing unusual about this; it has been the history in most cultures around the world. Even today, American Evangelists actually believe that woman is subordinate to man.

PARADIGM SHIFT

With the population explosion (in the last sixty-five years, India's population has more than tripled—going from 350 million to 1.2 billion), growing family sizes, general economic conditions in the country and mass movement of the population from rural to urban areas, the traditional joint family has rapidly disappeared in most parts of the country. With urbanization has come the need for women to work outside the home and that requires education for most nonmanual jobs. Simultaneously, due to enhanced communication and increasing education, women are becoming more aware of their rights, career options, and fairness and equality of opportunity in their work environment. The number of women in educational institutions as well as in the workforce is continuously increasing, especially in the cities. The proliferation of television and cell phones has played a great role in this development and also brought a certain Western orientation. As a result, at least in certain segments of the society, women have made tremendous progress in India. Today it is quite common to find professional women in high places like corporate board rooms, in the academia and politics, and as senior executives, physicians, engineers, lawyers, and entertainers.

So what does it mean to be a woman in India? There is no general, correct, or good answer to this question. It depends. And therefore, I will try to answer this question for two separate groups whose lifestyles and outlooks are exactly opposite of each other in many ways—professional middle-class women in the cities and the uneducated lower-class women in the rural areas.

The most important difference between these two groups, in a nutshell, is this: The educated city woman walks in step with or sometimes even a few steps ahead of her man. The uneducated village woman walks deferentially several steps behind her man.

PROFESSIONAL AND MIDDLE-CLASS WOMEN IN CITIES

Indian tradition bestows a certain *gender advantage* to women. In professional work environment, women are almost always treated with chivalry and respect. Unlike in the West, women were never considered as sex objects in India. On the contrary, there is a certain sense of purity and respectability to women often revered as images of goddesses. Here are some of the benefits enjoyed by women in this group.

- *Easier home life.* Indian professional women generally have a relatively easier home life due to the ubiquitous domestic help available quite cheaply. Unlike a professional woman in the West who must do every household chore by herself (sometimes with the help of the spouse when it is not football season or basketball season or baseball season or he is not out playing golf or drinking out with his buddies), dropping the kids at school, grocery shopping, cooking, and cleaning. More often than not, the Indian woman has servants to do all these and other tasks. In addition, frequently there is a mother-in-law (yuk!) or a mother at home, relatives or friends, and neighbors nearby, providing a support system that is simply unthinkable in the West. The flip side of this, of course, is the possibility of intergenerational conflict and the universal challenges of living with the in-laws, a problem women in the West rarely face.

- *Raising children.* Delivering and raising children is also a wonderful experience for women in this group because of the support system, long leaves from work, and the traditional pampering that women receive from all quarters. The negative side for the woman, of course, is the possibility of a little too much help and too much advice from the mother-in-law.

- *Performing arts.* In the area of the arts, cultural activities, and fashion, India is a paradise for the upper-class women. The diversity and quality of opportunities available to learn, practice, or just enjoy the performing arts like music, dance and theater, fashion design, and culinary talents is unmatched anywhere in the world. Indian classical music and dances have a unique, meditative aspect. The aesthetic Indian art forms have the most beautiful femininity at their root, the quintessential virtue of an Indian woman—delicate, fragile, elegant, and classy.

- *Fashion and clothing.* In terms of apparel, it is a paradise again with each Indian state presenting an extravaganza of exquisite artistry on cotton, silk, and raw silk. With the ever-so-innovative Bollywood, hundreds of new fashions are introduced every year to the delight of the discerning image-conscious woman.

WOMEN IN THE RURAL AREAS

There is a dramatic difference in the quality of life for the women in the villages in comparison with their sisters in the cities. Here the consequences of lack of education and the hypocrisy of the patriarchal, backward society are on their full inglorious display. To be a village woman in India is no fun. There are serious challenges to daily life caused by the problems of widespread poverty, poor sanitation, and lack of adequate basic facilities for health care and education. And a further aggravation is caused by their status in the society. A woman is always perceived as somebody's possession as a daughter, sister, wife, or mother with no independent existence of her own. The man is clearly the boss, and there is no pretense of equality. Superstition rules and life is often controlled by unbending dogma.

The village women's life is generally that of hardship where they toil shoulder to shoulder with the men folk outside doing manual work in the field and on the farms. Childbirth can be in the open area, under a tree or behind a bush, where the woman may take a couple of hours of break before she goes back to work. At home, there is no help; the woman must do everything herself as the men sit smoking, drinking, gambling, and bossing around. Physical abuse is common.

Change comes to rural India very slowly and girls' education is not the highest priority for most of the poor farmers. There are, of course, pockets of wealthy communities in the villages. Some of them may educate the girls but do not let them pursue independent careers. They are supposed be the decorated housewives, waiting on their husbands, and looking after the kids.

In many parts of the country, the dowry system still prevails, and one of the major tasks of a father is to save enough money and get his daughter married. This can be a formidable undertaking for destitute farmers, many of whom go into long-term debts ruining the entire balance of their lives. They cannot afford it; and yet tradition, peer pressure, false pride, and distorted concepts of "honor" force untenable and wasteful expenditure on gifts, celebrations, and dowries way beyond their means. Because of this financial drain of epic proportions, a girl child is almost always unwelcome in these families. Further, girls are thought to be not as strong or productive as boys and thus are much less of a help on the family farm. Finally, *"the girl has got to leave the house anyway, she is going to be somebody else's possession, her destiny will be controlled by her man, and she will be at her in-laws mercy so why spend on her and educate her? She is just a financial drain."* This is the thought process.

Yes, these are sad facts. But they are true. This kind of mind-set still exists in parts of India, and areas of the states of Uttar Pradesh and Bihar are particularly notorious in this regard. Blatant sexism prevails there, and local newspapers frequently report stories of barbaric behavior involving murders and burnings and the like, all caused by disputes about honor and dowry and gifts and unkept promises and alleged infidelities.

In the winter of 2011, the American television network ABC ran a series of special programs on the plight of girls and their families in certain segments of Indian society that will make every thinking Indian cringe and hang down his head in shame. The barbaric dowry system is a cancer on India that will not go away if the politicians and intellectuals continue to bury their heads in sand pretending that no problem exists. There is no substitute for immediate and severe punishment for the guilty.

There is a glimmer of hope, however. Social activists, NGOs, and certain government programs have taken up the cause of rural women. Micro-financing is taking hold opening up small business opportunities. Women's self-help groups are being promoted for activities in the areas such as community health, education, and alcoholism. Organizations like the Kasturba Trust are involved in great works of charity providing medical and social services to women in remote rural areas. However, from a national perspective, the overall progress is spotty simply because the population and its needs are so large. Clearly, much more remains to be done for the emancipation of women in rural India for visible, meaningful results.

In summary, the diversity of India makes it impossible to have a simple single answer to the question of what it means to be a woman in India. India is not Sweden and does not have the compactness, uniformity, and orderliness of an ethnically pure, economically advanced society. To be a woman in India can be absolutely great if you are an educated middle-class woman in one of the major cities. If not, life can be miserable.

India will never be a developed country until the lot of all its women is improved, until all women are treated with due respect and attain total parity with men in every walk of life.

NINE

The Last Thing India Needs

In 2008, industrial giant Tata launched its Nano, the world's cheapest car priced at $2,000. It was lauded as an engineering achievement comparable to man's landing on the moon. The Nano was a matter of great pride for India because it was built in the country using locally made parts and had a highly affordable price. However, environmental scientists have been skeptical of the car. Nano's projected sales have not materialized so far. With its lack of roads, parking spaces, and energy shortage, India does not need Western-style personal transportation. What it needs is better public transportation.

Dan Mayur

On January 10, 2008, at the Ninth Auto Expo in New Delhi, industrial giant Tata launched the Nano, its much ballyhooed ultra-cheap car. At a sticker price of $2,000 (the average car in the US now goes for ten times more at $20,000) the Nano suddenly brings car ownership into the reach of millions of Indians. It is supposed to give fifty miles to a gallon, is lightweight, and performs basic functions of a car. It is designed to fit four but can squeeze in five Indian people. It has no radio, no AC, only one windshield wiper and a small trunk space.

This event was widely celebrated as another example of India shining, the rise of India as a superpower, the new industrial leader, and a global economic power. India's need for being recognized as one of the big boys is so desperate that some in the media called the launching of the Nano an event comparable to man's landing on the moon. That many Indians will be able to afford to buy the Nano and will buy it is certainly true. And yet this is probably the last thing India needs.

THE PRIDE OF INDIA

There is no doubt that Indian engineers are second to none in the world, and it is to the credit of the Tata group and its technical team to come up with such a low-cost product. As an engineering achievement, this effort deserves recognition and applause. After all, the Nano has been fully designed and manufactured in India using totally indigenous parts. In this regard, it is certainly a matter of pride for India.

IN PERSPECTIVE

India, for its size and recent industrial activity, has probably the poorest infrastructure for road transport in the world. The road congestion, especially within the cities like Delhi and Kolkata and Bangalore, is worse than anywhere in the world with traffic moving at no more than a mile an hour during certain peak hours with a cacophony of ear-splitting honking all around. Air and noise pollution levels in most Indian cities are already at very unhealthy levels and would be unacceptable in other developed countries.

A broad perspective is essential to assess the overall impact of adding cheap cars to Indian roads with the intent of making them affordable to as many people as possible. Today there are approximately one hundred million motorized vehicles in India about 40 percent or so of which are passenger cars of every variety from the moribund Ambassadors and Padminis to shiny Lexuses and Mercedeses. The Indian auto industry is the seventh largest in the world. And while India has embarked on a program to build more roads, what exists and what is likely to happen in the foreseeable future seems to be totally inadequate for the needs. Here is some eye-opening statistics. Approximately one-third of accidental deaths in India are attributable to automobiles. For comparison, the US has four or five times more vehicles on the road and yet has less than one-third the traffic fatalities that occur in India. This is an indication of the quality and availability of the roads, driver education, and quality of the cars as well as technology under the hood. Does India really need more and cheaper cars under these conditions?

POTENTIAL PROBLEMS

Beyond road congestion, even a bigger problem in most cities will be that of parking where there is absolutely no space for this purpose in public places, business establishments, or residential areas. The population density in Indian cities is among the highest in the world. Regardless of the expected high mileage per gallon of gasoline, personal transport like this will always increase per capita energy consumption further pressuring demand and prices in energy-strapped India.

To meet the low price target, both safety and quality standards have to be compromised and lowered on a car like Nano. With Indian drivers—some of them incredibly erratic and reckless—Indian road conditions and reduced safety standards, the number of traffic accidents is sure to increase. This is a blessing to the notoriously corrupt Indian police as it will be to insurance companies. For a car like this, for a single male driver of twenty-five, by Western insurance standards, the annual premium could be well above the price of the car itself.

WHAT INDIA NEEDS

Nano's highly affordable low cost is a tribute to the competence and innovation of Indian engineers. It represents a great technical effort. However, a cheap personal car on its already crowded roads is not what India needs. This imitation of the West's ideas of material progress and personal success would be quite detrimental to India. What India really needs is an improvement in

Dan Mayur

public transportation providing more, better, cleaner buses and trains. It needs more and better roads and transportation centers to properly accommodate the vehicles it already has. With reduced congestion, the overall system efficiency will increase, and the costs will decrease. India absolutely does not need a cheaper car. Actually, countries like India need to make car ownership less attractive by increasing the taxes on them and making gasoline more expensive while simultaneously improving and promoting public transportation.

Where public transportation is not easy or possible, or in any case, as a complement to public transportation, private, personal transportation in the form of bicycles should be promoted as has been done so successfully in Western Europe. It is amazing to see the number of bicycles, special bike lanes, and bike-friendly road signs and street signals even in major cities like Copenhagen and Stockholm. It is not at all unusual to see even very senior corporate executives pedaling their way to the office not just in the summer but during the severe winters too. Five to ten kilometer commutes on the bikes are quite common and when needed, bikers are easily accommodated on the local commuter trains. This is what India needs.

Unlike Europe, India has tolerable weather conditions throughout the year, and bicycles would be particularly well-suited there. India does not need accident-prone cheap cars for which there is not enough gas, adequate roads, or room to park. More cars in India is not progress. It is an expensive giant leap backward. The West was fascinated by cars in the sixties, seventies, and eighties. Now it is looking at public transportation. It is strange to see that as the West is waking up to environmental, energy supply, and security challenges and trying to gradually wean itself from personal transportation like cars, developing countries like India seem to be moving in the opposite direction to repeat the mistakes of the West. The car has suddenly become a symbol of the changing India where the affluent class is aggressively pursuing American style individualism and personal happiness exactly at the time when America is painfully discovering that its high-energy-consuming lifestyle is unsustainable in the long run.

Chief UN climate scientist Dr. Rajendra Pachauri said,

I am having nightmares about the impact of this car.

Like Dr. Pachauri, I too have had those nightmares.

The first Nano rolled out of the assembly line in mid-2009. Since then, in over two years by the middle of 2011, reportedly only one hundred thirty thousand or so have been sold. As a matter of fact, during the first year of production, only thirty thousand cars were sold—not a terribly promising record for the cheapest car in the largest market. But this is not surprising for multiple reasons. First, the advertised $2,000 price tag was for the stripped-down version of this already minimalist car. The actual cost after taxes, delivery charges and must-add-ons in India like air-conditioning was almost doubled at $3,700, erasing much of its cost advantage over established cars like the low range Maruti starting at around $4,500. Second, there were at least six reported instances of the Nano catching a fire. And finally, it is the psychology of buying a car. In the Western world, the car is a necessity. In a country like India, it is at least as much a status symbol as a necessity, if not more. And somehow, a cheap, stripped-down little car just does not make a very impressive status symbol. Those who want to buy a car, have money. And people who have money want to buy a car that looks feels and acts like a real car.

The Nano may be an engineering achievement. But it is not a market-blazer and, in any case, India does not need it. Nano is a no! No!

TEN

Incredible India

POLITICS, BOLLYWOOD, AND BABA RAMDEO

India is a veritable kaleidoscope of humanity. It is the home of both the absurd and the sublime and everything in between. It is a land of contrasts. However, there are clear signs that India is on the rise. India's progress will not come through the efforts or the leadership of the entrenched corrupt politicians. Its future rests on the shoulders of four distinct groups—selfless patriots like Baba Ramdeo and Anna Hazare; educated technocrats like Nandan Nilekani and Jayram Ramesh; its tech-savvy, enterprising young people; and the ethical, visionary industrialists like the Tatas and the Jains.

The abnormal economic disparity existing in India where a two-billion dollar single-family residence coexists with the slums and shanty towns of the hundreds of million people living on less than a couple of dollars a day is well documented and amply discussed in various books, magazines, and newspapers. Interestingly, the same disparity exists in the beliefs, thinking, and behavior of the Indian people in almost all aspects of life. "*Unity in Diversity*" is a popular slogan here, but the diversity that exists from one extreme to the other is unreal.

Just consider Antilla, a rather strange-looking structure and the new home of the fifth richest man (net worth over fifty billion dollars) in the world. Mukesh and wife Nita Ambani live in this $2-billion home with their children. The twenty-seven-story, four hundred thousand square foot palace reportedly has seven elevators and a six-level parking garage and is said to require a service staff of some six hundred people. It is shocking to see the display of such conspicuous consumption that is Antilla in the context of the notorious slums of India where millions live miserably without running water and sanitation.

Not to be outdone by big brother Mukesh, sibling Anil Ambani and wife Tina are reported to be building an even bigger *swankienda* in the Pali Hills area, the Beverley Hills of Bollywood. Their supporters say, "If you got it flaunt it. If not the Ambanis, who will build such houses?" Maybe they are right, but here is a rambling thought in my mind. The purpose of a home is to keep the family close and together and provide a shelter. This can be done in many simple ways. Why does a small family of four or five need so much space? Families are defined by togetherness, and too much space creates distance, increasing isolation and thus defeating the purpose. It is not a question of wealth. Could anything else possibly be done with so much space and wealth, especially in a poor country?

But this is incredible India!

In one form or another, directly or indirectly, life in India today is impacted by the following four factors—business and political environment, organized or white-collar crime, entertainment, and religion.

In its economic development of recent years, India's new companies like the IT giants Infosys and Wipro have a lion's share as have the traditional leaders like the Tatas who run their businesses profitably but ethically and professionally. They make India proud. As India moves from its traditional agrarian to modern industrial economy and from rural to urban areas, such businesses are going to play a bigger and bigger role in Indian life. And yet there are numerous companies, small and large, like Satyam, that went belly up a couple of years ago, running fraudulent businesses, bribing bureaucrats, evading taxes, or turning out shoddy products and defrauding the public.

There are great charitable organizations like Pratham and Akshaya Patra, just to mention a few—doing absolutely outstanding work in literacy and basic education and supply of meals to schoolchildren, dedicated social workers like the publicity-averse, silent Gandhian reformer Baba Amte, enlightened philanthropists like industry leader Azim Premji, and literally thousands of NGOs working for the public good. Ambani built a two-billion-dollar home. Premji gave two billion dollars for education. India is an incredible mix of extremes, good and bad. Ridiculous and sublime. Greed and charity. Unfortunately, in India, the bad seems to trump the good more often.

This ancient land of 330 million gods has one of the biggest networks of ruthless mafia anywhere in the world. While such groups are usually very small in terms of number of people, their activities are far-reaching encompassing drugs, currency manipulation, human trafficking, and especially construction and land transactions that have seen an unprecedented boom in the last decade. It is a well-known secret that they have a symbiotic relationship with many politicians. In fact, politics and crime are almost synonymous in India, and for good reason. In his book, *Shantaram*, a partly autobiographical, partly fictional but mostly factual work, author Gregory David Roberts gives an excellent insight into Mumbai mafia and is a must read for any student of India.

In terms of basic necessities, life of the two hundred to three hundred million people in India's middle class has seen an undeniable improvement in recent years. India's economic strength and the much publicized GDP growth rates pertain to this group. The life of the remaining eight hundred to nine hundred million people has possibly worsened or remained stagnant at best. Rampant corruptions in public life, creaking and inadequate infrastructure, and unmitigated environmental pollution have put the quality of life for these people on a continuous downward spiral.

But Indians are a hardy lot known for their tolerance. They do not revolt. They do not complain. They have perfected two escapes to get away from it all periodically—entertainment and religion. For entertainment, Indians can immerse themselves for a few hours in the macho world of cricket, an unlikely national passion for a formerly enslaved country, or the vicarious dreamworld of Bollywood's mushy love stories and songs and exotic dances.

The other escape route goes through the temples of India. From Haridwar to Kanyakumari and from Rameshwaram to Banaras, Puri and Dwarka, India has been and is a highly religious land with innumerable festivals, pujas, and rituals. And to facilitate all that are hundreds of sadhus, swamis, gurus, babas, pundits, yogis, and assorted godmen—some genuine while others are pure charlatans. Religion can bring people together and unite. And it can divide people. But above all, religion brings hope to people. And life is sustained by hope as much as it is by food, water, and oxygen. It is a promise for a better tomorrow. It is a means for escape. It is a way to pass time. And in India, from the great temples of Tirupati and Madurai to the small idols of assorted deities placed under the neighborhood Banyan tree at the street corner, it is great business and great politics. Just for example, the Tirupati Trust is reported to have an annual income of 125 million dollars. Unfortunately, when religion gets intertwined with politics, political vested interests exploit the situation, causing rifts between different religious groups; examples of which are the violent fights that periodically break out between Hindu and Muslim fanatics due to political incitement.

INCREDIBLE CORRUPTION IN POLITICS

Today, in India, politics has nothing to do with public service. It seems like it is a career choice by persons of a criminal past. Political power provides substantial opportunities for wealth accumulation. The *Times of India* reports that as many as 304 members of Lok Sabha recorded an increase of personal assets by 300 percent during just one term of looting.

Even by Indian standards, 2010-11 has been the worst scandal-ridden period in India's sixty-plus years of history. During that year, the country suffered one humiliating shock after another—financial shenanigans of elected politicians in high places (the commonwealth games in Delhi, Adarsh Housing Society in Mumbai, 2G spectrum distribution in the ministry of telecommunication, the land and mining deals and other fraudulent activities by members of the Karnataka government, just to name a few) costing the nation hundreds of thousands of crores of rupees. One wonders how long this ingrained, systematic looting can go on.

The usual fate of these successive financial scams is that they get lost in the woodwork of pseudo, make-believe investigations since more often than not the superiors and other colleagues of the perpetrators and members of the judiciary may also be involved. Most of the problems get suppressed or forgotten, and the few that make it to the courts languish there for decades. So nothing really happens to the guilty. Life goes on. But how long will the public amnesia last? When will the chronic apathy end?

INDIAN POLITICIANS

Indian politicians are a most remarkable bunch steeped into the VIP culture that is unique to India. With some exceptions, it is a shamelessly privileged class unworthy of a nation where Gandhian philosophy and the teachings of the Holy Geeta are invoked at every opportunity. Indian politicians love moving around in motorcades with their large entourage of sycophants, their cars speeding around with flashing lights and deafening sirens, holding up traffic and disrupting street life.

Besides money, they love positions and titles, salutes and garlands, slogans, and speech-making inarticulate though most of them are. And they demand respect. These "servants" of the people act like royalty. They must be addressed with appropriate appellations like *Mahan Deshbhakta* (Great Patriot), *Janahit Samrat* (Emperor of People's Well-being), etc., and at the very minimum, by the mandatory "sir," an unseemly and slavish relic of the British Raj. It is unthinkable that an Indian politician will ever be called by a familiar lightweight name like Bill or Jimmy as in Clinton or Carter. If Clinton were an Indian politician, he would be addressed with the properly impressive *Sanmananeeya StreeHridayNayak Chirataroon Shreeman William RaoJi Jefferson RaoJi Clinton SahebJi*, as opposed to just the miserly "Bill Clinton."

SIRJI AND MADAMJI

As a matter of fact, in otherwise proud India, the servile "sir" and "madam" are even more common than the native suffix "*ji*" routinely used to show reverence. Anybody, however, low on the totem pole but in a position to do you a favor or hold up the approval or progress of anything you might be interested in, expects to be addressed by and gets addressed as sir or madam in addition to the mandatory bribe under the table. These designations typically follow the name as in Kapoor Sir or Nalini Madam. For a higher order sucking up, sir and ji can be used together as in "SirJi wants you right now. Hurry up."

Indian politicians love their birthdays to be celebrated in public with great fanfare. And they love their gigantic pictures displayed all over town. They love to see their names printed in huge block letters. Their passion for self-aggrandizement knows no bounds. There are hundreds of statutes of past national leaders around the country with plaques betraying this passion of present-day politicians. Typically, the name of the honoree whose statue it happens to be is inscribed in much smaller letters than the name of the politician in office who unveiled the statute. Here is an example:

Mohandas K. Gandhi
1869-1948
INAUGURATED BY SHRI XYZ JI
HONORABLE CHIEF MINISTER OF ABC STATE

A favorite activity of Indian politicians is to "cut a ribbon" to inaugurate anything and declare it open with their blessings. It is rumored that one of the politicians even had the gall to suggest that he had declared India's holy River Ganges open and ready to flow!

GERIATRIC POLITICIANS

India, the youngest country in the world with an average age of its population at twenty-five, has the oldest politicians with the average age of its cabinet at sixty-four and its head of government at eighty (compare this with the UK at forty-four, Russia at forty-five, US at fifty, and Canada at fifty-two). Of course, our current PM is so much younger than the alternative, Advaniji at eighty-three. Statisticians and scorekeepers need not worry. This will dramatically change upon the imminent coronation of Rahulji. One advantage of having geriatric politicians is that much of their misbehavior is confined only to financial fraud and not Clitonesque sexual shenanigans, for obvious reasons. They are too old.

CORRUPTION HONOR ROLL

As mentioned above, during the year 2010, a series of mega scandals broke out in India. Here is a partial list of alleged high-level corruption based on published reports in the national media. It is included here merely to illustrate the political environment existing in the country. It is emphasized that as of December 2011, the guilt of none of the individuals listed here is proven, and they may well be acquitted of any wrong doing. In that case, it would just mean that these selfless patriotic servants of the people had the opportunity for corruption but they remained untouched by the temptation and came out clean.

- *Mananiya Shri* (the honorable Mr.) Suresh KalmadiJi, head of the Common Wealth Games (CWG), marred by delays and alleged corruption. The cost of the CWG is estimated to be Rs. 70,000 crores (that is eleven zeroes after 7) or about $14 billion. Kalmadi is currently on bail after nine months of incarceration and is awaiting trial.
- *Mananiya Shri* Ashok ChavanJi, former chief minister of the state of Maharashtra and leader of the Adarsh housing scam, that allegedly involved misuse of funds and land allocated for the benefit of military widows. Chavan was forced to resign.
- *Mananiya Shri* Andimuthu RajaJi, former minister of telecommunications. The alleged fraud in the distribution of 2G spectrum is estimated to have cost the nation Rs. 1.7 lakh crores (that is eleven zeroes after 17) or about $35 billion. Raja is currently in jail awaiting trial. In early 2012, the Indian Supreme Court nullified all of the122 licenses fraudulently awarded by Raja.
- *Mananiya Shri* Bookanakere Siddalingappa YeddyurappaJi, former chief minister of the state of Karnataka. According to the local media, there were accusations of nepotism, partisanship, corruption, and profiteering. His pictures kneeling in front of the Godman Sai Baba frequently appeared in the local newspapers. He was forced to resign by his party.

The prevalence and the magnitude of the numbers involved in corruption are shocking. The decline in the value of the currency (one rupee is about two cents now), the economic growth of recent years, and the exploding values of real estate mean that the amount of money circulating both legally and illegally is so large that it easily takes nine, ten, eleven, or twelve zeroes even to represent routine underhand corruption transactions.

One does not have to be a revolutionary or an anarchist to wonder if Indian politicians have heard what happened to the czars in Russia. In their shameless greed and unabashed conspicuous consumption, are they not sowing the seeds of a major and bloody revolution in Gandhi's India? Indians are fond of movies, but no Indian movie matches what goes on in real life in the country. So will an AK-47 wielding, angry, young Amitabh start just shooting around some day? Maybe I am being an alarmist. I hope not. But if you love India, it is impossible not to worry.

Pankaj Mishra, a well-known Indian author, has insightfully analyzed the Indian electoral politics and the behavior of its politicians in his book *Temptations of the West*. He suggests that in India, electoral politics is a road to economic viability for undereducated demagogues, who once in office, seek only to secure their own financial future. They all seek power that in societies degraded by colonialism often comes without a redeeming idea of what it is to be used for. All they think of is enriching themselves without a broader view of service to the rest of the population.

The sad fact is that corruption is not confined to politics alone. It has now invaded big time in the Indian judiciary as well. Recently, the Supreme Court publicly chided the Allahabad High Court by saying "there is something rotten there" and that "nothing moves without money anymore." In the land of the Bhagawat Gita, this sorry state of affairs is further illustrated by the following:

- News item in *Times of India,* December 15, 2010: "SC judge puts ex-CJI in dock"

  New Delhi: Justice H. L. Gokhale of the Supreme Court has accused former Chief Justice of India K.G. Balakrishnan of misrepresenting facts to conceal sacked telecom minister A. Raja's attempt to influence Justice R. Raghupathy of the Madras High Court on behalf of two accused murderers known to the DMK leader.

Incredible India!

RELIGIOUS LEADERS

Indian politicians defrauding the nation and often connected with the mafia or involved in murders do not fail to play it to the masses by a display of their faith and religiosity. The newspapers frequently publish detailed reports of the worships and *pujas* (religious rituals) regularly offered by Indian politicians:

- News item in *Times of India* November 10, 2010: "Yeddyurappa Visits Rajarajeswara"

  Ahead of the no confidence motion in the assembly on October 11, Yeddyurappa had visited more than a dozen temples in Karnataka and even undertook to educate a boy who said he had prayed for the chief minister's victory in the assembly.

The BJP leader's favorite destination is the 11th century Rajarajeswara temple at Taliparamba in Kannur district of neighboring Kerala, said an aide of Yeddyurappa. Yeddyurappa had visited this temple and offered an elephant for the deity before taking office as the state chief minister in 2008.

- News item in *Times of India,* December 1, 2010: "Mukesh Visits Tirumala"

  Tirupati: Reliance Industries chairman and managing director Mukesh Ambani on Friday offered prayers at the famous hill shrine of Lord Venkateshwara at Tirumala here. He flew into Renigunta airport near here, from where he reached the shrine by road. After offering worship he left for Mumbai. Ambani donated Rs. 6 crore for gold plating of the sanctum sanctorum of the Temple.

INCREDIBLE BOLLYWOOD

Toward the end of the year 2010, a most welcome relief from the depressing daily barrage of political corruption news came from the titillating controversy over which one of the then sizzling chartbuster Bollywood dance items was better—"*Munni Badnaam Hui*" from the movie *Dabangg* or "*Sheila Ki Jawani*" from the movie *Tees Maar Khan*. I actually started receiving messages on my cell phone asking me to vote for "Munni." Some friends insisted I must choose

"Sheila." And I had no clue. My carefully cultivated ignorance hitherto date of all things Bollywood had been a major stumbling block to my progress up the social ladder in Indian high society. Recognizing that, and determined to change it, for my own edification and for the benefit of others uninitiated like me, I decided to do some research on this very important aspect of contemporary Indian culture. So here is what I learned about Bollywood dance, items, item numbers, and about "Munni," "Sheila," Madhuri, Aishwarya, and friends.

BOLLYWOOD DANCE

Bollywood dance is a mixture of numerous styles that include belly dancing, Indian folk and classical, Western popular, jazz, and even Western erotic dancing as in girls slithering down the pole in exclusive men's clubs.

The international appeal of Bollywood dancing is something that has been in the making for decades with affluent Indians immigrating to various parts of the world. It has now become popular in parts of Europe, and today, its appeal is rising in the US. Bollywood dance schools are now found in most major cities and wealthy parents enthusiastically enroll their kids in the hopes of raising the next Karina or Salman. Other than rhythmic, insistent pelvis-thrusting, sensuous, and energetic body movements, elaborate, glamorous costumes, and glittering jewelry are hallmarks of this dance.

The term "item" is commonly used to describe a catchy, upbeat, often sexually provocative dance sequence for a song in a movie. To a very great extent, the costumes used in the items determine the current fashion for the rich and famous.

An item number or an item song is a mandatory musical performance that has no relevance to the story or the substance of the movie assuming it has any. Its sole purpose is to display scantily or ornately clad dancing women and enhance the appeal and marketability of the film. The Indian audience feels cheated if there is not the full range of songs, dance, blood, and tears in the movie. Once they see all this, they indicate their satisfaction by joyous and spontaneous shouts of *"paisa wasool"* (Got my money's worth).

Item numbers are almost always available before the release of the movie. The early release creates curiosity, sets the buzz going, and advertises the movie way ahead of release. That also affords the filmmakers the opportunity to assess the market and shuffle songs as necessary and choose the ones with the best market potential. The female actor, singer, or dancer in an item number is known as an item girl. In a nutshell, an item in filmy slang is a sexy woman, with racy imagery and suggestive lyrics.

The item number is a much-awaited break in the movie greeted with enthusiastic loud whistles. Audiences absolutely love the abrupt and complete diversion from the plot, almost always a predictable, nonsensical, triangular love story dripping in mushy sentimentality about family values or patriotism, when a sexy babe begins to gyrate her rear end in sync with her entourage and a catchy tune blaring loudly in the background. Rhythmic music is a must and so are garish surroundings, sexy lyrics, and colorful garments.

People forget the plot and immensely enjoy the song and dance of the item number. In general, the item numbers have a far greater longevity in public memory. Despite hundreds of movies produced every year, item numbers like Madhuri Dixit's "Dola Re Dola" in the movies *Devdas* or Aishwarya Rai's "Kajraare" in *Bunty Aur Babli* are simply unforgettable for the true connoisseurs of Bollywood films.

The choreographers of these dances command considerable respect in the industry. Most notable among them are Farah Khan, Saroj Khan, Vaibhavi Merchant, and others. There are hundreds of popular item numbers, and everyone has his or her own favorite list. Based on the discussion with local aficionados, here is one possible list of the most popular:

Most Popular Item Numbers

	Item Song	**Item Girl**	**Movie**
1	"Sheila Ki Jawani"	Katrina Kaif	*Tees Maar Khan*
2	"Munni Badnaam Hui"	Malaika Arora Khan	*Dabangg*
3	"Dola Re Dola"	Madhuri Dixit	*Devdas*
4	"Kajraare"	Aishwarya Rai	*Bunty Aur Babli*
5	"Beedi Jalaile"	Bipasha Basu	*Omkara*
6	"ChhaiyyaChhaiyya"	Malaika Arora Khan	*Dil Se*
7	"ChhammaChhamma"	Urmila Matondkar	*China Gate*
8	"UP Bihar Lootne"	Shilpa Shetty	*Shool*
9	"Choli Ke Peechhe"	Madhuri Dixit	*Khalnayak*
10	"MehboobaMehbooba"	Helen	*Sholay*

Bollywood lovers are intensely passionate and partisan about their favorite items and item girls. A friend of mine canceled our long-planned dinner date upon seeing that this tabulation did not put his favorite Madhuri's "Dola Re Dola" in the first position. I am sorry, friend. This is what they told me; what do I know!

So on to the most important current national debate. The burning question was "Munni wins or Sheila? Who dazzles more on the Desi screen? Who is the bigger heartthrob? Who wins—the sexy bonanza called Munni Badnaam Hui, or the sensuous belly-juggler Sheila Ki Jawani?"

Bollywood experts were arguing everywhere about Munni's claim to bottom wiggling glory versus Sheila's. Some voted for Munni's raunchiness; others thought that Sheila's classic sexiness triumphed. I was torn between the two. I liked the doyenne of item numbers, Malaika Arora Khan, dishing out her sweetly nonsensical gibberish:

> Munni ke gaal gulabi; Nain sharabi
> Chaal nawabi re . . . ; Main Zandu balm hui, darling tere liye!
> (Whatever that means!)

But Katrina was simply irresistible in "Tees Maar Khan."

> My name is Sheila. Main tere haath na anee; I am too sexy for you!

Wah, wah! Kya baat hain!

Incredible India!

INCREDIBLE SHINING LIGHTS: BABA RAMDEO AND ANNA HAZARE

So this incredible India, with its corrupt politicians and failing judiciary, great scientists and talented artists, incomparable history and rich culture, creaking infrastructure and dysfunctional government, teeming population and dismal poverty, this complex and confusing land of mind-boggling contrasts, where does it go from here? What is the future of its 1.2 billion people half of whom are below twenty-five years of age? What is its rightful place and role in the family of nations? And how does India progress to that place as a nation?

Just maybe, there is hope. Happily, there are selfless, dedicated patriots in India like Baba Ramdeo and Anna Hazare among others who may have an answer. Baba Ramdeo is no run-of-the-mill swami of whom there are thousands and Anna Hazare is no ordinary social activist of whom there are thousands too.

BABA RAMDEO

Ramakrishna Yadav, popularly known as Baba or Swami Ramdeo, is an enlightened modern-day yogi. He is known for his efforts in popularizing Yoga as enunciated in Patanjali's Yoga sutras. He is also one of the founders of the Divya Yog Mandir Trust headquartered in Haridwar that aims to popularize Yoga and Ayurveda. The *New York Times* calls him *"a product and symbol of the New India, a yogic fusion of Richard Simmons, Dr. Oz and Oprah Winfrey, irrepressible and bursting with Vedic wisdom."*

Baba Ramdeo is a patriot, an inspiring public speaker, Ayurvedic medical expert, and a Yoga guru par excellence all rolled into one. Over eighty-five million people follow his Yoga camps via TV channels and video. His Yoga teaching sessions are free for all. This thinker, philosopher, motivator, proud nationalist seems to be the real thing that India needs desperately at this time. He proposes to restore India to its old glory through Patanjali Yoga, Ayurveda, education, and renaissance of national pride. Two thousand years ago, Patanjali, an Indian sage and the father of Yoga, compiled a blue print for living a complete, moral, and spiritual life based on the science of Yoga.

The eight elements of his approach for a complete and perfect life are:

1. Yama—Prescriptions on how to treat others: no violence, honesty, no stealing, no lust, no possessiveness.
2. Niyama—Personal discipline and responsibility: cleanliness, contentment, austerity, study of the wisdom of the scriptures, awareness of a superpower.
3. Asana—Physical fitness and mental stress relief.
4. Pranayama—The science of breathing; the care of the heart and lungs.
5. Pratyahara—Withdrawal from external influences.
6. Dharana—Concentration.
7. Dhyana—Meditation.
8. Samadhi—Absolute bliss.

THE PATANJALI YOGAPEETH

Swami Ramdeo's flagship project, the Patanjali Yogapeeth (PYP) Trust, was inaugurated in 2006. Its aim is to build the world's largest center for spirituality, Ayurveda, and Yoga that includes a teaching university and facilities for treatment. The trust offers free treatment to those who cannot afford to pay. For others, treatment is provided at a lower cost than at commercial hospitals. Through the PYP, Swami Ramdeo works with various institutions and medical organizations in an effort to study and improve the effectiveness of yoga for the treatment of diseases like diabetes, hypertension, obesity, etc. He has also opened an Ashram on an island off the Scottish coast for the convenience of his European followers.

Beyond Yoga, Swami Ramdeo, a proud patriot, has dedicated himself to the cause of India. He is a driven man with a clear vision and an urgent mission of nation-building through individual development based on yogic principles, awareness, and education.

NATIONAL ISSUES

Baba Ramdeo has raised a number of national issues through his yoga camps. His focus is on change in the governance policies of India and the lifestyle of the common people. Some of the most important issues are as follows:

- *Bharat Swabhiman Campaign.* Baba Ramdeo has initiated a movement named *Bharat Swabhiman* (Pride of India) with the intention of eradicating corruption, crime, and poverty and transforming India into a world power. For this effort, he plans to enroll up to a million members in each district. Baba Ramdeo does not seek any political position for himself.
- *Malpractices in the agricultural sector.* Baba Ramdeo believes that the use of fertilizers and pesticides has led to an undue load on the meager resources of farmers and increased profits for large businesses involved in the trade. This poses a big threat to farmers and to the health of the common man since the farmland and crops are becoming contaminated with harmful chemicals.
- *Consumption of fast-food and soft drinks.* Baba Ramdeo is concerned about the increased consumption of fast and packaged foods and

soft drinks by Indian youth. He believes that these products are disease-causing and generally harmful.

- *Exploitation of farmers.* Baba Ramdeo has great empathy for the Indian farmer. He believes that corrupt governance practices are responsible for the miserable conditions of the farmers and other backward groups in the society. Agriculture is the biggest contributor to India's economy and yet the farmers seem to be the most poverty-stricken class.
- *Indian black money in Swiss banks.* Indian money stashed away illegally in Swiss banks is estimated to be between $1-1.5 trillion. Baba Ramdeo demands that the nation must recover it immediately.
- *Seven hundred million Indians living on less than a couple of dollars a day.* Official surveys indicate that at least seven hundred million people (60 percent of the population) are living on two dollars or less a day. Improving their lot must be the first priority.

Baba Ramdeo's movement has received considerable traction and support among the Indian youth angry and frustrated by the failures of successive governments on the national scene. Baba Ramdeo has joined forces recently with another patriot and proud Indian, Anna Hazare, who has made the eradication of corruption in public life as the sole purpose of his life.

ANNA HAZARE

Kisan Baburao Hazare, affectionately called *Anna* (respectful designation for an older brother), a confirmed bachelor and, at sprightly seventy-four, is a social activist. Recently he has been in the limelight as the prominent leader in the anticorruption movement that has caught fire in India in early 2011. His movement relies on nonviolent methods based on the teachings of Mahatma Gandhi. Anna was instrumental in the development of Ralegon Siddhi, his ancestral town and a village recognized as a model for its self-sufficiency and environmental design. Anna was honored with *Padma Bhushan*—one of the highest civilian awards—by the Government of India in 1992 for his efforts in Ralegon Siddhi.

Frustrated by years of rampant and blatant corruption and government inaction to arrest it, in 2011 Anna Hazare went on an indefinite hunger strike in order to exert pressure on the Indian government to enact a stringent anticorruption law. Anna's team of activists proposes a *Jan Lokpal Bill,* for establishing an ombudsman with the power to deal with corruption in public places. The fast led to nationwide protests, sort of an *Indian Spring*, in support of Hazare. The fast lasted almost two weeks ending only after the government accepted to discuss Anna's demands in the parliament. There are many versions of the anticorruption bill, of course, and in what form Anna's bill finally winds up in the machinations of Indian politics is anybody's guess. One thing for sure, this humble man from rural India, with no formal education and who started his career as a flower vendor and ended it as a veteran of the Indo-Pakistan wars, has had a profound impact on Indian politics. He has aroused the nation like no one has in recent years.

It is not surprising that Anna has been ranked as one of the most influential people in India by the national media. He has always been an activist looking out for the little guy. In the early 2000s, Anna Hazare's efforts led to the establishment of the Right to Information Act (RTI), a powerful tool available to any citizen. It represents a giant stride toward enhanced transparency in government. He has now embarked on the mission of electoral reform. Admittedly, Anna has been controversial as are most reformers anywhere in the world. The wealthy and entrenched establishment rarely supports change. It thrives on the status quo. Indeed, the rich are doing well in India. The poor do not know and do not care. The middle class is squeezed, frustrated, and about to blow up. And that is where reformers like Baba Ramdeo and Anna Hazare derive their strength, get their inspiration, support, and following.

The Anna Hazare movement is for real. Certainly, there are extremist fringes on all sides in politics. One of the criticisms is that his insistence on his version of the anticorruption bill amounts to blackmail, that he does not understand or care for constitutional issues. But this is an extraordinary situation and extraordinary situations call for extraordinary solutions. After all, corruption is not constitutional and has grown unchecked into the 2G, CWG and Adarsh Housing monsters under the watch of the current leaders of the ruling party—ManMohansinghJi and SoniyaJi and RahulJi and whoever is next-in-the-lineJi. The unconstitutionality is irrelevant here. The fact is that every popular uprising seems to be unconstitutional to the ruling party.

Using the late Vaclav Havel's (ex-president of the Czech Republic) words, the Hazare movement represents the "power of the powerless." It illustrates the unrelenting struggle for dignity, social justice, and fairness for the ordinary citizens. It demonstrates common man's solidarity against decades of systematic corruption and embezzlement of public funds. Undoubtedly, this movement will result in a positive change. It may not eliminate corruption, but it is a step in the right direction. It has already created awareness among the masses. It is educating people. It has helped them understand their rights. In some ways, it is empowering the common man. It will apply brakes to the rampant, run-away corruption.

MANAGING EXPECTATIONS

The real problem, it seems will be managing expectations about the anticorruption legislation and the impact of the Jana Lokpal. The danger is that the average Ramoo on the street might expect too much, a dramatic change in his life, in his future. No, that is not happening any time soon. India is not going to become Sweden.

Removal of systemic corruption is a process. It is not an event. It is not like finding one Sadam Hussein, one Bin Laden and killing him. Corruption is everywhere, at every level, in every walk of life in India. It will take decades to eradicate it fully because it requires a change of mind-set. But what is needed now is a quick, severe, visible punishment of a few high-level miscreants to set the tone and give the assurance to the common man that the system is changing, that there is justice, that there is hope. In this regard, what happens to Kalmadi and Raja is a real test of India's justice system.

WHERE IS THE REAL PROBLEM?

Movements like those launched by Anna Hazare and Baba Ramdeo, to mobilize the youth to clean up the system, remove corruption, and make it more open, fair, and efficient are heartening. But politics and politicians are a reflection of the society. They do what the people do in one form or another. And the fact is that in India today, in almost every walk of life, an average citizen faces some form of corruption and, knowingly or unknowingly, willingly or unwillingly, participates in it. In a sense, we may all be called corrupt. If bypassing the rules in private life is acceptable, it seeps into public life. So what is this movement about corruption and against whom? We cannot effectively change India without changing ourselves. In his excellent column in the *International*

Herald Tribune (July 1, 2011), journalist Anand Giridharadas makes a powerful argument. Anand writes,

> The overwhelming tone of this rage (against corruption) is "us versus them." The "us" is the ordinary people of India, the "man on the street," as they too-literally call him here—hardworking, diligent, scrupulous; the "them" are the bums in politics and the bureaucracy—lazy, deceitful, imperious scoundrels . . .

> The blame cannot so tidily be placed on the "them." This may well be an "us" problem as much as a "them" one, in which case the revolution being called for will have to be a revolution within.

Clearly, Indians are in hurry to get ahead. The every-one-for-himself philosophy is taking hold. Our public and private behaviors are different and inconsistent. Our social culture ignores, accepts and knowingly or unknowingly promotes corruption by breaking rules, ignoring authority, taking shortcuts. We are the enemy.

Anand's argument is indisputable. Sloganeering, saluting the national flag, praising the wisdom of our scriptures, bragging about the ancient culture, and invoking the name of Mahatma Gandhi whenever possible is what Indians do consistently and with remarkable hypocrisy. The bigger challenge and the real salvation are in actually translating the underlying ideas into personal behavior. Until then, the greatness of India will remain purely fictional.

So this is India. Incredible India! The land of the Antillas and slums. Of Patanjali Yoga and Bollywood item numbers. Of mafia and philanthropists. Of corrupt politicians and dynastic rule. Noble and absurd. Ritualistic and modern. Confusing. Complex. Diverse. Poor but proud. Dynamic. Youthful. Struggling. Fun-loving, Carefree. Trying to make its mark. With a lot of hope and potential. And with equal number of problems, obstacles, and uncertainties. One can only hope for more Swami Ramdeos and Anna Hazares and pray for their success. But we all must change ourselves too.

THE SALVATION

Indeed, through the dark clouds of corruption and despair, there are rays of hope that are beginning to shine through. It is clear that the current crop of potbellied, chair-grabbing, money-loving, dynasty-worshipping geriatric politicians will continue to loot India until they die or are defeated. India's salvation will come from four distinct groups:

- Selfless patriots like Baba Ramdeo and Anna Hazare
- Highly educated technocrats like Nandan Nilekani and Jayram Ramesh
- The tech-savvy, go-getter, proud, ambitious, enterprising young people of India now flourishing in places like Bangalore and Hyderabad
- The ethical, visionary industrialists like the Tatas, the Premjis, and the Jains, just to mention a few

There are so many problems. There is so much potential.

Incredible India!

ELEVEN

Entrepreneurship in India

THE MISSION OF BHAVARLAL "BHAU" JAIN

India's future will be shaped by its selfless social activists, its highly educated technocrats, its tech-savvy youth, and its entrepreneurs like Bhavarlal "Bhau" Jain. Starting with humble beginnings in rural Maharashtra, this visionary industrialist and community leader has demonstrated that ordinary villagers can deliver extraordinary performance. Furthermore, he has shown that one can conduct ethical business in India without compromising his values. An ultimate patriot, Bhau is dedicated to uplifting the local population using local agriculture-based resources with environmental sensitivity and focus on sustainability. He has converted the arid countryside in Jalgaon into a heaven on earth. Bhau is a role model for the future leadership of India.

S ome people are born great; some achieve greatness while greatness is thrust upon some. Shri Bhavarlal Jain, affectionately called *"Bhau"* (elder brother) by thousands of his friends, admirers, and employees is a giant among contemporary Indians who have achieved greatness by their vision, enterprise, and extraordinary hard work. The New India of tomorrow will become a reality because of the entrepreneurs like Bhau.

Bhau's incredible rags-to-riches life story from his very humble beginnings at Wakod in rural Khandesh to the pinnacle of industry and subsequent recognition at the highest national level in India has been amply documented. He has been filmed, photographed, interviewed, written about, and honored numerous times in prestigious national media and business publications. That his life is a uniquely inspiring success story and that he is a modern business leader par excellence is thus very well-known. However, even at the very personal level, Bhau is a wonderful human being approaching the Vedic ideal of *"Purushottam"* (the best man defined in the Hindu Scriptures, the Vedas). Besides being an entrepreneur, he is a thinker, a writer, a philosopher, a teacher and a coach, a guide, a student ever eager to learn new things, a motivator, an innovator, a philanthropist, and a community leader. And he is a loyal friend, proud father, and a very loving grandfather. He immensely enjoys all these roles and carries them out with remarkable distinction.

It is only by a stroke of good luck that one comes across and gets to know people like Bhau for there are so few of them. Fortunately, every few years, during my periodic visits to India, I get an opportunity to visit and spend some time with him. Even through these brief and infrequent encounters, certain aspects of his personality become immediately evident. His life is an open book of profound wisdom from which we can learn a lot. So here is the Bhau I know as an everyday human being and some of the things that impress me most about him.

VISION

If I were to describe Bhau by just one word, out of numerous possibilities, the one that jumps up in my mind is "visionary." Big things come out of big ideas, and Bhau is a man of big dreams. As Stephen Covey says in his celebrated *Seven Habits of Highly Effective People*, first things first—begin with the end in mind. Bhau has an intuitive feel for where he wants to go, and everything he has done in his exemplary career of over forty years has been with a single-minded focus on his vision. He wants to begin by helping the local economy. He wants to do it scientifically through the development of industry, be it plastic pipes and sheets, irrigation systems, or food processing. He wants the business to be agriculturally based, utilizing local resources in order to maximize benefits to the region. He wants to do it on a large scale and, of course, ethically.

Not ambition but low aim is crime—Bhau has taken this adage to heart and put it in action. "If Tatas can do it, why can't I? If America can do it, why can't we do it right here, bigger and better?" This is the essence of his thought process. Bhau's broad long-term vision is a flourishing Khandesh, an industrial Maharashtra, a developed and globally respected India. To his credit, Bhau recognized before most experts that judicious water management for irrigating the over forty-three million hectares of nonproductive, barren land was the key to the success of the nation. Continuously expanding the area covered by drip irrigation, the so-called Second Green Revolution is a significant part of this vision. He proudly calls himself "son of the soil" for agriculture is his true passion.

WORK ETHIC

Bhau is a man of action with an incredible get up and go. Once his vision is set and his mind is made up, no obstacles, neither the Indian bureaucracy, nor persistent health issues can deviate his mind or energy from the pursuit of his vision. It is this work ethic and personal discipline that helped Bhau fight off the pain and anxiety of no less than four heart procedures at a relatively young age. Bhau does not indulge in empty talk and meaningless political discussions, a common practice in India. He is a practical, serious, scholarly man not given to display of emotion or celebration without achievement. He believes that work ethic defines character, and character defines the man, not his worldly fame. Bhau leads a very clean, simple, and principled life with no indulgences and no vices. A wonderful example of his emphasis on clean life is the fact that workers at the Jain factories get a glass of healthy milk and banana rather than tea and samosas during their snack breaks. He has a well-planned daily routine that he follows scrupulously. He works hard and expects others to do so. Work is indeed worship for him.

EXCELLENCE

The first thing you notice when you see or visit anything pertaining to Bhau—any of his offices, his factories, his laboratories, his gardens, or his farms—is his pursuit of excellence. Clearly, Bhau believes that if something is worth doing, then it must be done well. There is no better example of this than his residential/business complex in the enormous sprawl of his fabulous property at Mohadi, which could easily be the envy of the Ambanis and Bachchans. In just a few years, he has converted the dry wasteland on the outskirts of Jalgaon into a literal "*Nandanvan*" (a heavenly garden). Everything about him is first-rate. He is an A-plus man running an A-plus operation so much so that all his children and grandchildren have names starting with the alphabet A. This is not an accident. It is the vision. It is the dream. It is the expectation. Surely this must put considerable pressure on the youngsters to perform in the A-plus manner. But so far, nobody has disappointed. Bhau's pursuit of excellence is also manifest in his heroes and in the people he surrounds himself with. Jawaharlal Nehru is his political hero. J. R. D. Tata is his ideal business leader. There can be no better role models to follow. And among his friends are people like poet Mahanor, sculptor Sudhir Deshpande just to name a couple among the ranks of artists, writers, professionals, politicians, and business people all excelling in their own fields. Bhau understands the value of people and their relationships.

CONTINUOUS IMPROVEMENT

It seems to me that one of the most important keys to Bhau's success is his focus on continuous improvement in personal life as well as business practices. Bhau keeps up with the developments in the advanced countries, both in technology as well as management techniques and aggressively adopts those suitable and appropriate for his businesses. I have a distinct recollection of one of his medical visits to the US in the early eighties. Personal computers, in their really primitive form, had just started coming out. Even the most sophisticated US businesses were not using the PCs then. When Bhau heard about the Apple LISA during his trip, he asked his assistant to learn as much as possible about it, see how the Jain Group could use it and then go ahead and buy it. And he did. I was stunned. Needless to say, today the Jain Group has a very modern IT center fully equipped with the best equipment. Bhau is a voracious reader and has an impressive collection of books in his personal library. Innovation, on-going research, making the most of limited local resources, waste minimization, and an insatiable thirst for knowledge are the drivers of continuous improvement in Bhau's approach to life and business. Calculated risk-taking is also a part of Bhau's continuous improvement process. A wonderful example of this is his underwriting the financial guarantees for up to five years when he first introduced the drip irrigation system to hesitant farmers unfamiliar with the new technology.

PRINCIPLE-CENTERED LEADERSHIP

Family-controlled large business houses have existed in India for decades, and many of them have been very successful and profitable. However, ethical practice has never been a strong point of Indian business. The Jain Group stands in shining contrast to this unfortunate fact thanks to Bhau's principle-centered leadership. Bhau has injected his personal values of honesty and integrity to the fullest in his businesses, a rare accomplishment in the Indian business environment. Bhau deals with people from all walks of life, in all kinds of positions in public and private sectors. His friends range from master politician and strongman Sharad Pawar to loyal friends Rajabhai Mayur and Sureshdada Jain representing a very wide spectrum of personalities and attributes and yet Bhau deals with them with equal ease and naturalness never compromising his basic principles and values. Deeply founded in the Indian philosophy and culture, Bhau is immensely proud of his background, his parents and his early childhood influences. He has a clear sense of his roots, his calling, and his destiny. He derives much of his strength from this clarity.

PHILANTHROPY

Bhau's philanthropic activities under the auspices of the Jain Foundation have been well described in the numerous books and articles written about him. He is now dedicating more and more of his time for community leadership and charitable activities starting his efforts right in his birthplace of Wakod, to Jalgaon, and beyond to other places in the region. His emphasis, as always, is on education, health care, and making employment/business opportunities available to deserving people. He is a frequent speaker at formal and informal functions and his speeches are most informative, interesting, and inspiring. That itself is a major community service in motivating and guiding young people. He is an activist for the farmers and is a strong supporter of low-interest loans and price-floors for their products.

HUMILITY

The personal trademark of this high-achiever is not a Rolls-Royce, a Rolex watch, or diamond-studded gold cuff-links. The most strikingly visible characteristic of Bhau is the ever-present smile and his almost unbecoming humility. This unassuming man literally shines in his simple, clean attire, pleasant manner and friendly conversation. He is, indeed, "Bhau" to everybody in the true sense of the word.

WALKING THE TALK

Bhau is a man of few words and more action. He does not preach. He demonstrates things by doing them. He shows by personal action. He walks the talk. The true legacy of a great leader is to train and leave behind him people better than himself. Bhau has raised, trained, and developed four wonderful sons—Ashok, Anil, Atul, and Ajit—all highly successful business professionals in their own right. And Bhau did this not by force, not by direct demands or in any way lecturing, controlling, or constraining them. True to his philosophy, Bhau leads them by example. Bhau says, "If they can see your actions and behavior, why do you need to tell them anything?" What a refreshing thought for those of us prone to giving long, deafening lectures to our innocent children. Bhau is a team player and believes that the future belongs to those who think collectively, consult, and cooperate. And consistent with this approach, all major business and family decisions are taken jointly under Bhau's unobtrusive guidance.

FOCUS ON EDUCATION

Notwithstanding Bhau's impressive success in the business arena, developing local economy, and providing employment, his magnum opus is undoubtedly in a noncommercial area. Bhau has always felt that the most important and urgent need in India is that of quality education and leadership development. With that in mind, in the year 2007, Bhau embarked on the project closest to his heart—establishing a unique boarding school that offers a wonderful balance of academics, extracurricular activities, athletics, the performing arts, and spirituality all with the intent of producing ethical, proud patriotic leaders of tomorrow. Today the school, Bhau's favorite "Anubhuti" flourishes with its beautiful buildings spread over a sprawling lush green campus on the hills of Mohadi on the outskirts of the city of Jalgaon. Bhau is at his happiest in the company of the twelve—and thirteen-year-olds, and it is a joy to watch this giant of industry completely lose himself and become one of them. They, in turn, love and worship this humble man as a beloved and respected grandfather in the family.

In early 2012 Bhau topped off all his career achievements with the establishment of the world-class Mahatma Gandhi Research Center in the sprawling Jain Hills Complex.

In summary, Bhau is an enlightened businessman and civic leader with a purpose. His personal mission is based on five cornerstones—gratitude for the local people, patriotism, social responsibility, promotion of agribusiness, and leaving a legacy for future generations and community. In his famous "Psalm of Life," Longfellow says:

> Lives of great men, all remind us
> We can make our lives sublime
> Departing leave behind us
> Footprints on the sands of time

Bhau will be with us for many more years. But he has already changed the world around him for the better. He has created giant footprints on the sands of time. Bhau has been instrumental in bringing the Second Green Revolution to the farmlands of India with more than 60 percent and ever-increasing drip irrigation coverage. This is a landmark achievement worthy of the Ramon Magsaysay Award or the Nobel Prize for Peace. On January 26, 2008, Bhau was awarded the honorary title of "*Padma Shree*" (one of the highest civilian awards) by the president of India.

Bhau is a role model for the new breed of leaders India needs. The future rests on the shoulders of enlightened, visionary entrepreneurs like Bhavarlal Jain.

AMERICA

The Statue of Liberty, New York
Welcoming immigrants to the land of opportunity

TWELVE

Life on Four Wheels

Many of America's socioeconomic problems today are self-created. An integral part of the much-coveted American way of life is possession of a car for personal transportation and a large house in the suburbs. More than a hundred million Americans drive to work alone every day. Only about 5 percent of the workforce uses public transportation. This is an inefficient use of energy and also a cause of the current problems of health, environment, and the economy. For long-term sustainability, public transportation must play an important role in individual lives and the national economy.

Dan Mayur

From television news and talk shows, to radio, newspapers, and magazines, American media are abuzz with talks, discussions, and debates about the faltering economy, sluggish job market, escalating energy prices, deteriorating environment, and controversial health-care legislation. Media talking heads, academic pundits, and politicians of all stripes and color are pointing fingers at each other and proposing solutions from one extreme to the other for deficit reduction and balancing the budget, stimulating the economy, and creating jobs, tax reform, alternate energy, environmental protection, and so on. Despite this heavy intellectual turmoil, there is no agreement, no solution, and no consensus on any issue of significance, except for the pronouncement that the American way of life must be preserved.

Governments are fond of statistics and regularly generate all kinds of numbers. They are nicely compiled, tabulated, and filed away. Few people read them. And fewer yet reflect on them or do anything specific with them. The US Census Bureau makes a periodic assessment of various population parameters. Its 2010, American Community Survey released in September 2011 offers a look at life on four wheels detailing how the country's 137 million workers travel to their jobs and how long each trip takes.

Life on Wheels in America in 2011

Category of Workers	%
• Drive alone	77
• Carpool	10
• Use public transportation	5
• Walk	3
• Other	5

Average one way travel time: 25 minutes

Most people scanning through the newspaper might cursorily glance at such tabulation as an idle curiosity before moving on to the more important sports section to check on how badly the local Wolverines massacred the visiting Daredevils. It seems to me, however, that a great majority of the problems ailing America today are reflected in this little tabulation. These simple numbers tell you why Americans are obese, why we are always short of time

130

and rushing, why we are permanently stressed and have health issues, why we have an energy crisis, why our infrastructure is crumbling or is inadequate, how we gobble up a disproportionate amount of the world's resources, and why the one thing everybody agrees on—the desire to preserve the American way of life—may not be achievable in the long term. This small tabulation tells a big story of the American way of life and the American economy.

OBESITY AND OTHER HEALTH ISSUES

Medical professionals estimate that almost two-thirds of American adults and one-third of their children are either overweight or obese. This is not surprising if more than three-fourths of the working population is driving alone, sitting in a car for almost one hour every day just going back and forth to work. And this does not include other discretionary or leisure driving. The suburban dream homes that we so much long for are a major cause of American obesity, besides, of course, rich foods and humongous portions. People who live in the suburbs do not walk. Every little errand requires the use of car. The initiated few among them, who want some exercise drive to a health club, go round and round to find the parking spot nearest to the entrance and pay to get on a treadmill for thirty minutes of walking. Have you noticed that city dwellers are slimmer and fitter than suburbanites? You have to walk in the city as people do all over Europe.

The problem of obesity in America now is way beyond being just an aesthetic or "good looks" consideration. As a precursor to high blood pressure, diabetes and heart disease it is a major health care and cost issue, and that in turn means lost work time and additional costs for you and your employer. Besides being a potential cause for obesity, rush-hour driving in heavy traffic causes considerable stress and anger in the drivers, and stress and anger have their own unhealthy side effects.

ENERGY CONSUMPTION

According to the US Environmental Protection Agency (EPA), each year the United States produces about 10 percent of the world's petroleum but consumes about 26 percent of the total global production. Cars and light trucks are the single largest users of gas, consuming about 43 percent of the total petroleum usage. Overall, cars and light trucks consume approximately 16 percent of the total US energy used.

Americans recognize that they are dependent upon imported energy, some of which must come from unfriendly nations that can control the supply and pricing. Thus the energy security issue also is a national security issue with a significant bearing on America's foreign policy. Americans are a very innovative people, and there is no doubt that they will eventually come up with alternative energy solutions to replace at least a large portion of imported energy to reduce the dependence on others. But in addition to alternate energy, the greater need is for alternate transportation solutions different from the one-person one-car formula. Today the world population is seven billion. The world has no place or energy for seven billion cars. The long-term solution must lie not in more cars or more energy but in more fuel-efficient public transportation.

The Census Bureau Survey shows that 77 percent of the 137 million workers drive alone. That means about 105 million cars have only one passenger. Just for the sake of argument, if half of these single drivers start carpooling or using public transportation, fifty million cars will get off the road saving 150 million gallons of gasoline or over $500 million daily ($180 billion annually). With such reduction in driving come several tangible and intangible benefits like reduction in traffic congestion, travel time, environmental pollution, and road and car maintenance needs, number of accidents, police and wrecker calls, not to mention the wear and tear and stress on the drivers and subsequent doctor visits and hospital stays. It is one big snowball effect.

ENVIRONMENTAL POLLUTION

Automobiles have a major impact on the environment. According to the EPA, "Driving a private car is probably the most polluting daily activity an average citizen performs." While great progress has been made in reducing air pollution from automobile exhaust over the past decades, motor vehicles still account for a significant amount of environmental damage. The pollutants in the exhaust are oxides of nitrogen and volatile organic compounds causing ground-level ozone or smog leading to respiratory problems, carbon monoxide that is poisonous and also causes smog, carbon dioxide considered to be responsible for global warming, and particulate matter. The amount of pollutants generated is directly proportional to the number of vehicles on the road. In addition to air pollution, automobiles also cause water and noise pollution and generate considerable solid waste. It is common sense that we need to prudently minimize the number of cars on the road and our driving.

THE REAL PROBLEMS

Americans love all things personal as in a personal computer at home, personal trainer in the health club, and personal coach at the school. American individualism, as wonderful as it is in many ways, seems to have gone way beyond its optimum as far as transportation is concerned. As stated earlier, one hundred million people driving to work alone using personal transportation, their own cars, is the nationally most expensive example of this obsession. Continued and insatiable demand for energy is not just a cost issue, but it is also a major environmental and a national security issue.

"Drill Baby Drill" is a popular Republican chant. It betrays environmental insensitivity and blindness induced by considerations of short-term profitability and the demagogic need of pandering to special interest groups during the election cycle. Energy supply considerations also influence the nation's foreign policy and create the need for trying to find weapons of mass destruction or regime change in the oil-rich areas of the world. A minute of reflection reveals that more energy in whatever form—alternate or conventional, fossil or non-fossil fuels, imported or domestic oil, more roads, more cars, better cars are not and cannot be a part of any sustainable long-term solution. The real solution is to reduce personal transportation, cut down on the number of cars, drive less, develop and use public transportation. We do not need more energy. We need fewer cars. Unfortunately, few Americans want to hear this, and fewer politicians want to talk about it.

Personal transportation as it is used in the so-called American way of life is one of the most wasteful things devised by man. But then, there are so many other things that are wasteful in America not the least of which is the size of American homes. In most suburban areas, even middle-class houses are routinely four or five thousand square feet in area, almost always occupied by aging empty-nesters or soon-to-be empty-nesters. Cooling and heating these large and partially occupied houses, frequently poorly insulated, is a major drain on the nation's energy resources. Restaurant serving portions are big and getting bigger taking the nation's average waistline with them. Restaurants want to make more money, so they sell you more and charge you more. They design every portion with the intent of packing some of it in a doggie bag. I say make the portions smaller and cut the price.

Dan Mayur

LONG-TERM UNSUSTAINABILITY OF THE AMERICAN WAY OF LIFE

If supersized restaurant portions, cars, houses, and waistlines are representative of the way of life that Americans have been historically accustomed to, it is most unlikely that this lifestyle can be sustained in the new globalized world. At 312 million, the US represents less than 5 percent of the world population of seven billion. And yet the US uses more than one-fourth of the world's petroleum production. It was OK when underdeveloped India and China were practically dormant. These sleeping giants have woken up now, and together make up 40 percent of the world's population. Unlike in the past, they are global players now, aspire to a higher standard of living, need a bigger share of the world's energy and other resources, and are willing and able to compete for them.

In the globalized world with technology and knowledge, capital, goods, services, and people flowing freely across borders, it is naïve to think that a lopsided use of resources can continue forever. Nor can the disparity in the standards of living or compensation levels between the people who can trade with each other freely go on unchallenged. Just as an example, a qualified engineer in India, doing excellent work makes about $1,000 a month. His exact counterpart in America doing the same quality work makes ten times that, $10,000. Elementary market arbitrage tells us that this is unsustainable in the long term in the globalized, mobile world where everything can flow across borders.

There will be a built in tendency for convergence and the forces toward equilibrium will put an upward pressure on the Indian salaries and a downward pressure on the American salaries. Admittedly, this is a gross oversimplification of complex economic issues. But it illustrates the point and provides an explanation for why China and India are hiring while America has been firing, why their growth rates are in double digits, and why the US is struggling to hover around 2 and 3 percent. Americans are innovative, intelligent, and hardworking people. America will always be a world leader, and Americans will continue to enjoy a decent lifestyle. But yesterday is permanently gone. And tomorrow will not be like yesterday. The fact is that the American lifestyle has been bloated. Americans will have to lower some of their expectations, trim down the fat in various aspects of their life, and tighten their belts in more ways than one.

THE ROLE OF THE GOVERNMENT AND THE PEOPLE

Americans may be in a state of denial. America is not an island. To the extent that globalization has made the world interdependent, it must accept and understand that now we progress or falter together with other nations. The world resources are not unlimited, and no nation has the right to claim and consume a disproportionate share of these resources. Individually, we must become extraordinarily conscious about energy efficiency and become sensitive to the environment. Whenever possible, double up, carpool, combine errands, minimize discretionary and leisure driving; support, promote, and use public transportation.

But people need easy access to safe, convenient, and affordable public transportation and making it available is the job of the government. It is true that Americans are too far down the road in their lifestyles and urban planning that is entirely too dependent upon personal transportation. But that is simply unsustainable in the long run. Any transition will be painful, but it is a question of survival. It will take a nonpartisan, visionary policy, and some hard, temporarily unpopular decisions that may involve substantially increasing gasoline and road taxes, making parking difficult and expensive and generally making single-person car driving less attractive. It will require reduction in new highway construction but a much greater emphasis on public transportation in the form of vans, buses, light rail, and even significant incentives for carpooling.

New transportation planning for the future is easier. Modifying and revamping the existing systems will present considerable challenges to American innovation and resolve, at least in some cities. It is recognized that with the exceptions of a few, most American cities are very large in size, spread out widely with varying zoning laws and population densities. They were primarily and consciously laid out to be served by controlled access highways, a situation completely unlike the walkable centers of European cities. Nevertheless, the prevailing one-car-one-person equation is still a losing proposition. In such cases, if full-blown public transportation gets to be prohibitively expensive, carpooling and shared vans and minibuses can provide effective alternatives.

In any case, promoting and developing public transportation is a clear case of the *pay me now or pay me later* admonition.

THIRTEEN

Musings on Religion

Religion plays a significant role in people's lives throughout the world. After the September 11 attacks on the World Trade Center in New York, religious issues have come to the forefront in sociopolitical discussions even in countries not directly affected by terrorism. Much of the posturing has been against Islam. Lack of education and bigotry has exacerbated religious strife. In a fundamental sense, all religions seek the same thing—peace, happiness, and salvation for mankind. Understanding and tolerance are keys to religious harmony. A basic introduction to all major religions and their holy scriptures such as the Bible, the Koran, and the Geeta should be a required part of the education system.

T he World Trade Center attack of September 11, 2001, was a turning point in contemporary human civilization and ushered the world into a new era of strife, awareness, and debate on religion. While each religion may have minor differences within its various sects or subgroups, much of this global struggle has been perceived as being with Islam—it is Islam versus Jews in the Middle East, it is Islam against Hindus in the Indian subcontinent, and it is Islamic terrorists attacking various targets all over the Western world. There are some who suggest that this is the beginning of a war of civilizations, although only a handful of miscreants are involved on the Islamic side. Notwithstanding the existence of religious fanatics in many parts of the world, fortunately there is enough sanity among intelligent, reasonable people who do not condemn an entire religion because of the acts of a few and do not call this aberration as a war of civilizations. There is no war on Islam. It is against terrorists and terrorism.

RELIGION IN THE WEST

Bigotry resulting from the lack of education, communication, and exposure to other cultures seems to be the main cause of religious hatred. Whether we are religious ourselves and whether we wear our religion on the sleeve is immaterial. The fact is that religion is a reality and many people all over the world take their religion very seriously, and some even do it with a sense of superiority. In many countries, religion plays a far bigger role in the common man's life than the intelligentsia would like to believe or is comfortable with.

Europe has spectacular church buildings, but they are empty. They just want peace there, not a show of their faith. But Americans, especially with the resurgence of its religious right in recent years, are crowding their churches and make a major display of their faith. Is Obama a Christian? Incredibly, this was one of the "most important" subjects of discussion in America during his entire first term in office until the media talking heads found something else, equally trivial, to agonize over during the 2012 election primary season when Mitt Romney, a Mormon, began to lead the field of eight Republican aspirants. Are Mormons really Christians or is it just some cult? This became the burning question of the day.

RELIGION IN INDIA

Religion has always been an integral part of the Indian culture. With its beautiful, large, and small temples, innumerable *gurus* and *swamis* and a growing extravaganza of religious festivals from *Janmashtami* to *Ramnavami* to *Ganesh Chaturthi*, to *Holi* to *Durga Puja, Dassera,* and *Diwali,* religion has assumed the greatest ever importance in India. And it is the same thing in the Islamic and Christian worlds. For the unenlightened masses, belief in the superiority of their own faith is natural. And if you have lost a loved one due to a cause that maybe related, however remotely, to any kind of perceived religious conflict, your thinking about the other religion is all the more likely to be irrational.

EDUCATION FOR RELIGIOUS HARMONY

How do we cope with this very unpleasant fact of life? By saying religion is taboo in public discourse for the sake of political correctness? By trashing one group's feelings in favor of the other's? Should political correctness always trump logic and reason? I would propose exactly the opposite. To the extent that much of the hatred comes from lack of education and ignorance, you would want to discuss the issues, understand the causes, and help people overcome their prejudices by knowing, understanding, and learning from each other. And if a certain group happens to have the wrong image, it can only be erased by communicating, explaining, and educating. I think a basic introduction to all major religions and their holy scriptures—the Bible, the Koran, and the Geeta should be a required part of high school curricula all over the world.

Inasmuch as the world's attention is focused on Islamic terrorists, the Islamic scholars and community leaders have a great responsibility in this regard to aggressively and visibly draw the line to separate their communities from the few terrorists that might be hiding amongst them. They should do so by loudly condemning them, cornering them, and eliminating them. So far, there is no visible and widespread evidence of this. Perception is reality, and the ordinary people all over the world need to see a clear rejection of terrorism from the Islamic community at large.

RELIGION AND GOD

Religion has a purpose. It is intended to bring people together, provide an outlet for their spiritual needs and give purpose and meaning to their life. Religion has been instrumental in promoting, supporting, and nurturing human creativity and the arts—music, sculpture, and painting. And religion is at the forefront of many charitable organizations. And yet, despite all its intentions and the potential good it can do, organized religion and religious wars have brought a lot of grief and misery to humanity over the centuries.

Religion can unite and religion can divide people, and so there is a natural tendency among a certain class of intelligentsia to reject all religion. But the concepts of religion and God are interrelated.

The concept of God arises, most likely, from human mortality and the fear of death. At least some people find the concept convenient to explain birth and death. God is a convenient resort when cause-effect analysis hits a stonewall. When one rejects religion, one rejects God. Very simply, there are believers and there are nonbelievers. For the believers, there is something out there in whatever form, shape, or name one chooses to give it, some force, some power, some energy that controls human life, or at least, it has some influence on it. And there is a reward for the good deeds and a punishment for the bad deeds. For the nonbelievers, everything is a statistical random occurrence.

PASCAL'S WAGER

In discussing religion and God, it is interesting to consider Pascal's Wager. This may be especially important for the scientists among us with their emphasis on logic and reason. Named after the French philosopher, mathematician, and physicist Blaise Pascal, the Wager suggests that, even though the existence of God cannot be determined through reason, a person should wager as though God exists because living life accordingly has everything to gain and nothing to lose. This concept is easy to understand with the help of the well-known simple decision matrix of probability theory.

IF YOU DO BELIEVE IN GOD

a. And God actually exists. Great, you got it made with infinite gain.
b. But God actually does not exist. No harm done, nothing lost.

IF YOU DO NOT BELIEVE IN GOD

    a.   And, in fact, God does not really exist. Well, there is no loss or gain.

    b.   But if God does exist. Watch out! You may be in deep trouble.

Look at the odds. Prudence dictates that it is in your own interest to believe in God and behave accordingly. For a scientist, this is the only rational position.

Historically, Pascal's Wager was groundbreaking as it had charted a new territory in probability theory, it was one of the first attempts to make use of the concept of infinity, and it marked the first formal use of decision theory. Indeed, nature follows certain laws. Science can try to understand and explain these laws but can never tell you why they exist and why in the particular form they exist. Why does the apple fall to the ground? It is the law of gravity, of course. And why does the law of gravity exist? And why does it involve the masses of the two bodies and the square of the distance between them in the specific relationship that it does? I do not know and neither do you. Even the scientists accept it as a fact of nature since reason and logic reach their limits rather quickly and are unable to explain everything observed in nature.

As a matter of fact, most scientists including Newton and Einstein and even the quantum physicist and Nobel Prize winner Feynman of our times are known to be believers. Now, what God you believe in and in what shape and form, if and how you display your religiosity, or otherwise what you do with it, is strictly a personal matter. Even in the current or historical strife that is customarily blamed on it, religion itself has been less of a problem than its misinterpretation and bigotry of the extremists who clearly miss the point.

Religion is and should be a strictly personal matter.

FOURTEEN

America at Crossroads

America has been the undisputed leader and a force for good in the world for over a century. However, even in a flourishing, successful nation decadence can set in if its citizens take their good fortune for granted. They could become complacent, lose motivation, and develop self-righteousness that leads to social and political arrogance. In the past two decades, these tendencies have become widespread in the American society. This is because of several political and cultural reasons. America is at a critical juncture. It can still regain its position of leadership by returning to its basic values of fairness, hard work, and liberty and justice for all. Its constitution and great universities are America's real strengths as are the basic decency and the innovativeness of its people. With discipline and will power, America can get back on track.

For most of the last century, America has been the economic, military, and moral leader of the world, an unmatched object of admiration around the globe and a powerful magnet for immigration. People in other countries still aspire to the American way of life, look at America as the land of opportunity, and want to be a part of America. And for the most part, America welcomes them. But today, things are beginning to look quite different. America itself seems to have been overcome with self-doubt.

> According to recent surveys, nearly 70 percent of Americans believe that the country is headed in the wrong direction. It is not geography that is in question, but rather our national purpose, spirit, credibility and competence. Central to the wave of unease and negativity surging throughout the country is the realization that the values and virtues that made America a source of strength, stability, and inspiration throughout the world are now in disrepair. Our falling dollar and soaring budget and trade deficits reflect the overindulgence of our appetites; and neglect of prudent fiscal planning, discipline, and savings.

These shocking words are not those of some disgruntled anti-American leftist. They come from two individuals whose patriotism is beyond reproach. It is what former US senators William Cohen (Republican from the State of Maine) and Sam Nunn (Democrat from the State of Georgia) say in a highly thoughtful article in the December 30, 2007, issue of the *Boston Globe*. They continue,

> The absence of sound fiscal, tax, and energy policies has eroded our international competitiveness and subjected us to regional instabilities and to the pricing policies of oil cartels and authoritarian leaders who are eager to flex their new muscle. Our leadership in science and technology is challenged by powers in Asia and Europe as we debate the validity of Charles Darwin's theory of evolution. While these and other challenges demand serious attention, our political process seems determined to engage in games of trivial pursuits.

These words written four years ago describe today's national situation perfectly. Things have not changed. As a matter fact, they have gotten worse and continue to deteriorate. Certainly, Cohen a former secretary of defense, and Nunn, a former chairman of the Senate Armed Services Committee, both individuals of stellar reputations and commanding bipartisan respect, know what they are talking about. However, in my opinion, what they are pointing out are mere symptoms of some really fundamental problems with the evolving American culture. The issues outlined by Cohen and Nunn in their very thoughtful article pertain to four categories:

- Lack of competence and credibility of the US government
- Disrepair and inadequacy of physical and human capital
- Declining US competitiveness in the global market place
- Increasing energy insecurity of the US

It is easy to blame unpredictable terrorism, illegal immigration, unfair trade practices of emerging powers like China and the collusion of oil-producing countries for these problems. While such factors could possibly exacerbate some of the problems, they certainly are not the cause. The current untenable situation is self-created with root causes deeply ingrained in the contemporary American culture. This situation has been developing and festering over a long period of time.

Like so many before me, I landed on the shores of America some forty odd years ago seeking higher education, professional opportunity, and socioeconomic fairness. As an aspiring and thankful immigrant, I felt that life was pretty good. America seemed to have all the values, all the decency, all the serenity, and all the quality of life that one would ever want. I got what I sought and more. I had made the right decision. This was the greatest country in the whole world.

Unfortunately, the seeds of decline are frequently embedded in the success itself. Nothing goes on forever. Even the tallest trees do not grow to the sky. Throughout human history, the greatest civilizations also have gone through the inevitable life cycles of growth and decline. The loss of competitiveness in international markets, the ongoing economic turmoil, and a depressing outlook for the future in the minds of ordinary citizens in recent years makes one wonder if this is the onset of America's decline. Have Americans taken their good fortune for granted and become complacent, lost motivation, and developed self-righteousness? Have they become socially and politically arrogant? It would seem that in the past two decades these tendencies have become more visible in the American society. Both, the drivers and the

145

manifestation of the arrogance, complacency and potential decline are evident in the following aspects of American political life today.

POLITICS

No principles, no convictions. American presidential campaign politics in its incredibly long, two-year period presents the ugliest spectacle of name-calling, spinning, distorting, and mudslinging even at colleagues within the same party. This is absolutely unworthy of a civilized and developed nation. Winning at any cost seems to be the governing mantra in politics as it is in business or sports or anything else. Americans are obsessed with being number 1. Winning at anything and everything is the governing philosophy. What is so shocking is that competitors in primary elections, after viciously attacking each other, without principle or conviction, can just as easily get into bed with each other upon the slightest enticement of any kind of a reward. During every election cycle, you see this happening, and there are numerous examples, the most glaring of which is George Herbert Walker Bush attacking Reagan's economics as unworkable voodoo and then raving about it after Reagan asked him to be his running mate.

RELIGION

A current phenomenon in American politics is the dominance of ultra-right-wing fundamentalist religious groups, their unabashed pandering by certain politicians, and the resultant hypocrisy about separation of church and state. The fact is that in recent years, religion and politics are increasingly intertwined. David Campbell and Robert Putnam present an excellent analysis of the impact of religion in their book *American Grace: How Religion Divides and Unites Us*. Some of these ultra-right wingers do not seem to be very different from Islamic fanatics in their extremism. It is most interesting that Europe's churches are being deserted as the ranks of American churchgoers are expanding. Columnist James Carroll, writing in the *International Herald Tribune*, talks about the difference between the US and Europe:

> In the very years that majorities of Europeans were walking away from organized religion, they were resolutely turning away from government sanctioned killing, whether through war or through the death penalty; they were leaving behind narrow notions of nationalism, mitigating state sovereignty, and, above all replacing

ancient hatreds with partnership. All of this stands in stark contrast to the United States, where the most overtly religious people support the death penalty, the government's hair-trigger readiness for war and the gospel of national sovereignty that has made the US an impediment to the United Nations.

GUN CONTROL AND CRIME

One more example of political opportunism is the appeasement of the National Rifle Association. Gun control is an area where the otherwise desirable American pursuit of individual freedom has gone absolutely berserk. The country was rightly indignant over the killing of three thousand Americans by terrorists on 9/11. Unfortunately, the fact is that Americans are killing Americans daily in larger numbers in drive-by shootings, crimes of hate, crimes of passion, family disputes, petty thefts, anger at society, mental derangement, or whatever, all facilitated by easy availability of guns. The US sometimes displays a remarkable capacity for not learning and remains the only country in the civilized world not to have sensible gun control laws for the safety of its people. No place, no town, and no neighborhood in America are safe. Undoubtedly, the US is the most violent country among the developed nations of the world.

OPPORTUNISTIC FOREIGN POLICY

American foreign policy has been another area that has gravely tarnished the American image. The view from overseas has been particularly uncomplimentary in this regard. In the past several years, I have had the opportunity to travel all over Europe from Oslo to Rome and from Helsinki to Zurich. In informal discussions over a glass of wine or cappuccino with professional friends, intellectuals, or people in general, what you hear is a strong rejection of any war and disapproval of any intervenist American policy for the so-called nation building. Obama has achieved a degree of success in reshaping the American image hardened by experiences and memories of the past. America now talks about winning hearts and minds. The wounds, however, are so deep that it is going to take a long time to change this unfavorable image.

With all the lofty words about democracy and freedom, historically American foreign policy tended to be opportunistic, supporting dictators and autocrats like Musharraf of Pakistan and the Saudi kings and seemed to be totally oblivious to the consequences of its military action on innocent civilians.

We rightfully mourn the deaths of the three thousand American servicemen in Iraq. We call them American heroes. That is fine. But the fact that six hundred thousand—plus civilians, mostly children and women, died in Iraq gets simply brushed aside as "collateral damage that happens in a war." Was that not really a kind of mass destruction that resulted from the search for the fictitious WMD?

When it is necessary, revolutions happen in the world, despotic rulers get thrown out, people liberate themselves, and free nations are formed. India threw out the British, the Iranians got rid of the Shah, the Russian and the French revolutions happened. All these succeeded without American help. The world does not need unilateral action from another country to liberate it and enforce foreign values upon it.

ISRAEL AND TERRORISM

There is really no denying that throughout its existence, Israel's intransigence has been the major cause of the Middle East turmoil and America's unwillingness to make Israel see reason has been the primary reason of terrorism against the West. However, America can still restore its position of respect and leadership in the world by recognizing and supporting the role of the United Nations, fully pulling out of Afghanistan and other parts of the world, and getting Israel to respect international law and agreements. This will yield a double bonus of reducing the debilitating drain on the US treasury caused by war-related military expenditures, help cut the budget deficit, and simultaneously reduce terrorism. Visible American presence overseas motivates and incites the terrorists. The Obama administration has had considerable success in eliminating certain key terrorist figures. But the terrorist organizations are amorphous, spread to many parts of the world, and are very unpredictable.

At least now, ten years after 9/11, the US policy makers must recognize and accept that military might will never eliminate, reduce, or even control terrorism. In the nonconventional, asymmetric warfare, tanks do not work. This recognition can result in considerable savings in the strained national budget.

The only approach that might work in combating terrorism is focused aid to cooperating nations for educating their youth in order to improve the quality of life for them and added expenditure for enhanced border security for the US. A very painful and expensive legacy of terrorism is the brute force approach we have adopted for airport security. It is aggravating and wasteful of time and human resources, and surely, there is a lot of room for more innovative and effective solutions.

While one can enumerate all the problems with the government and politics, it is important to remember that the government is a reflection of the society at large, especially in a free and democratic country like the US. You get the leaders you elect and the government you deserve. So the problems of politics and foreign policy derive from the expectations and attitude of a majority of the nation's citizenry, as do the socioeconomic and quality of life issues. Here are some of the current cultural problems with the American society. Recognition and acceptance is the first step. Americans are sufficiently resourceful and perfectly capable of solving these problems for themselves.

CONTEMPORARY CULTURAL ISSUES

MEDIA

Once hailed as a major innovation, the twenty-four-hour news with its muckraking, focus on trivia, and constant bombardment of the same news regardless of its significance does more harm than good. The incredible coverage of a relatively minor event like the Iowa Primary and its nonstop analysis by the pundits makes one think as if God was descending from the heavens. In the summer of 2011, in the Iowa Straw Poll for Republican candidates, out of the six hundred thousand registered voters, some thirty thousand voted and Michelle Bachmann got five thousand of those to win the nine-candidate race. This utterly trivial event was enough for the media pundits to regurgitate the news and its profound analysis with the fervor of the second coming of Christ nonstop for the following four weeks. And it is the same thing whether it is a political event, a scientific discovery, a celebrity mischief, or one of the many and frequent mass murders like school shootings in the country. Venom-spewing radio talk shows especially like those of the religious right hosted by the Rush Limbaugh ilk represent yet another low in the social dialog and have no redeeming value whatsoever. The ever-increasing audience support of such talk shows is shocking and does not augur well for America.

WASTEFULNESS

Blessed by great natural resources and their own hard work, Americans have enjoyed a very high standard of living for over a century. And judging by the much lower standards of many of the other countries, American affluence may appear wasteful to some. A glance at people in other cultures or other countries and you begin to think how fat Americans are, how big their cars are, how large their houses are, and how huge their open spaces and parking lots are compared to those in any society anytime anywhere in the world. For a long time, this, in fact, was the beauty and attraction of America.

You begin to notice how thick and bulky local newspapers are (because of advertisements, not news), how much junk mail gets stuffed into the mail boxes, how large the restaurant meal portions are, how much of the disposable plastic and paper products American use, and how much garbage they produce. With all the current talk about environmentalism and energy, American lifestyle may be the most wasteful in the world, plundering away the world's resources like there is no tomorrow. In this regard, globalization may have a mixed impact on certain countries in the world. Americans will keep on importing cheaper resources from the developing countries eager to make a sale. This will permit continuation of the American orgy but deplete the exporter's resources in the long term. In the short term, of course, this creates employment and brings in income.

UNFETTERED CONSUMERISM

Unfettered consumerism and commercialism are integral parts of American affluence, and this is most blatantly evident during the extended Christmas period. Christmas now starts in the nation's malls in October, full two months ahead of time. In this supposedly "religious" country, Christmas has lost all its meaning and sanctity as sale-crazy consumers lose all their sanity stampeding the store gates enticed by "Free TV for the first five customers. Store opens 4 AM." America is becoming a country of middle men whose only goal in life is to sell, sell, and sell. From junk consumer goods to household products, insurance, real estate, investment ideas, snake oil, youth potions, diet pills, their own companies, and themselves, people in America are always selling, advertising, and promoting something 24/7. After the terrorist attacks of 9/11, the president of the country asked everybody to go shopping! There was no call for sacrifice. No plan for increasing taxes to fund the expensive war on terror.

An unintended consequence of such single-minded consumerism is that people do not want to do anything without a profit motive. At the micro level, this causes everyone to be for himself with a short-term focus and shallow relationships. At the macro level, trend-oriented, maniacal trading can create winners and losers, ever increasing the gap between the rich and the poor. While one can praise the virtues of unrestrained capitalism and free markets, such gaps inevitably produce social discontent and increased crime for which eventually the entire society pays a very heavy price.

BORROWING AND SAVING

The greed and desire to possess every material good that is produced and promoted in order to keep up with the Joneses has created a new class of people in today's American society. In most places in the world, people belong to one of two simple classifications—"the haves" and "the have-nots," economically speaking. Not so in America. Here, these two classes do exist, but they are getting ever so smaller. In between the two has emerged the third and the largest class of people who "have but have not paid for it" types. People want everything and borrow for everything: house, car, appliances, education, vacation, wedding rings, anything at all (except for caskets and burial plots) are available on "buy now pay later" or "no interest payment for four years" basis. Everybody wants to give you a loan, offers you a great payment plan, and help to consolidate all your loans at a great interest rate. This is the way of life that vote-seeking politicians promise to preserve. This is the way of life that all economists have been saying is unsustainable. Just like the people are burdened by debt, the US government is overextended as the current economic crisis testifies. The American people and their government have been living beyond their means for a very long time. This story cannot have a very happy ending unless serious measures are undertaken urgently without political agendas and bickering. Such serious measures mean austerity where necessary and stimulus when needed.

America needs a cultural shift toward saving from today's rampant borrowing and spending mind-set. Prosperous happy societies of Europe like Germany, France, Sweden, and Belgium have household savings rates of 10-13 percent.

Asians are known to be inherently thrifty. In contrast, today the savings rate in the US hovers around 3-4 percent after having reached zero in 2005. The US also has a much heavier promotion and ease of accessibility of credit cards compared to the rest of the world. Shopping is promoted as a civic duty, something to do for your country. It is hard to believe that buying one more TV for the bathroom or an extra shirt that you do not need can bring about long-term progress and happiness to the country and qualify you as a patriot.

INSATIABLE CORPORATE GREED

Corporations and governments are formed and staffed by people and reflect the disposition and the mind-set of the people running them. Since the bursting of the technology bubble in the year 2000, the American financial system has been beset by one mega-scandal after another primarily due to the actions of unscrupulous banks and other financial institutions wrecking retirement portfolios and destroying lives of innocent people. And yet the twenty-million-dollar bonuses and one-hundred-million-dollar executive severance packages continue without shame or restraint.

The prevalence of corporate greed and malfeasance is so high that it almost seems like a conspiracy of the rich against the poor, of the haves against the have-nots, of the highly educated elite against the ordinary citizens. For a common man, it has become impossible to trust anything or anybody in the financial world. The Obama administration has taken measures to add checks and balances and improve transparency in the system, but clearly that does not seem to be enough.

The "Occupy Wall Street" movement in the fall of 2011 is a serious grassroots expression of public anger. Corporate fat cats should consider this as a serious wake-up call and shape up in a hurry. There is an unmistakable global trend here. The Arab spring of 2011 has started a revolution to bring down long-entrenched despotic dictators in the region. A seventy-four-year old obscure, unpolished social activist named Anna Hazare has mobilized millions of Indians in a movement to curb widespread, high-level corruption in India and bring the culprits to justice. America does not have political despots, and it does not have third-world type rampant corruption. But here we have elite, highly educated white-collar criminals armed with complex financial algorithms. They are openly and royally screwing the public while pretending to be safeguarding their nest eggs. They better watch out because the American Fall now follows the Arab Spring.

THE ENTERTAINMENT WORLD AND EDUCATION

Reports after reports point to the decline of American competitiveness and academic achievement in math and science by high school students. Among other reasons, one of the most important causes of this, in my opinion, is the mindless obsession with professional sports, TV, trashy rap music, and action-packed movies and the virtual deification of the athletes or entertainers who receive absurd compensation and, more often than not, are extremely poor role models for America's youth. The dominance of this entertainment and professional sports business in American life helps make the adults potbellied couch potatoes and the children lazy dreamers interested in get-rich-quick schemes. The lure for easy money and unrealistic expectations has helped to destroy the traditional work ethic that made America, America.

The lack of interest and motivation of American high school students is the result of the prevailing education system and the generally poor quality of teachers. America, the world's richest country, ranks at a miserly twenty-sixth in the quality of its education system, way behind smaller nations like Finland and Korea. It is shocking to see that 25 percent of American kids drop out of high school before graduation. Only 22 percent of the children in high school eventually graduate from college and very few of them with math and science majors. The compensation of American school teachers is poor compared to teachers in places like Finland where teaching is considered a profession on par with medicine and law. In the recent misdirected efforts at cost cutting, school funding and teacher compensation has come under great pressure. Is it really all that hard to figure out what America's real problems are and what it means to its future?

Education and health care should never be profit-making businesses or cost-cutting targets. They should be looked at in their proper perspectives as investments in the future of the nation and in the health and happiness of its citizenry.

FAMILY VALUES

The core of any society is the family unit from which everything emanates. Cultural, religious, and moral education starts at home. Ethical and patriotic values are instilled and nurtured at home. In most cases, personality and behavior problems start at home and thus can be solved at home to a large extent. Two career families, latchkey children growing up with TV and video games, consumerism and the urge to keep up with others, the urgency to get ahead at any cost, and the aggressive pursuit of individualism and personal gratification of the "Me Generation"—all these have taken a heavy toll on the American family. The Beaver Cleaver family, once the American role model, has now become irrelevant. American public policy and social systems need to be refocused on the family while awareness, education, and conscious behavior modification are essential at individual and family level. European-style childcare and women's rights and equality issues are worth considering in this regard.

HOW THE WORLD VIEWS AMERICA TODAY

The current burning issues in America are its stagnant economy and creation of jobs to alleviate the pain of unemployment stuck at 9 percent. While every pundit and politician has his solution, the fact is that there is no silver bullet because this is the consequence and cumulative effect of several political and cultural factors mentioned above. Here is what two distinguished journalists from two very different parts of the world see. Roger Cohen writes in the *International Herald Tribune* on November 1, 2011:

> Globalization and the information technology revolution are sucking away jobs; the jobs that remain demand levels of education that the country is doing a poor job providing. Debt, national and personal, hangs like a giant cloud over the United States. Other nations are growing so fast that the US share of global output fell to 3.5 percent in 2010 from 4.6 percent in 2000. The country is beset by paralyzing political division. Growing inequality has trampled on fairness to the point that Americans are taking to the streets. Right now America is neither morally compelling nor materially convincing.

Santosh Desai, writing for the *Times of India* on November 8, 2010, sees America this way:

> The US has always been a country obsessed with its own image, but till such time as it served as the world's biggest engine for new ideas and enterprise, the rest of the world had much to gain from it. It is only in the last few years that this American self-absorption is beginning to turn sterile. The world's romance with the idea of America is on the wane.

THE UNMATCHED STRENGTHS OF AMERICA

The foregoing litany of problems brings into focus the current situation in America but by no means portends its demise. Almost all these problems are temporary and fixable. America the beautiful is still close to being the proverbial Garden of Eden—a majestic land of beauty and bounty with more natural resources than any other country, with a human spirit and can-do attitude unparalleled anywhere in the history of mankind.

More than 150 years ago, in the middle of the nineteenth century, French traveler aristocrat Alexis de Tocqueville wrote about America's greatness. Among other things, he observed and eulogized the equality, middle-class aspirations, spirit of free enterprise, and the sense of the possible in the American culture.

Here are some of the major strengths of this *"land of the free and home of the brave."*

The Constitution. The most enviable thing about America is its remarkable constitution and the respectful adherence to it by the political establishment. Politicians come and politicians go, times change, and national crises arise. This wonderful document has withstood the test of time over two centuries and remains a beacon, a guiding light to its systems and institutions.

Universities. The second most important thing going for America is its research organizations and universities. These are unparalleled in resources, scope, and quality anywhere in the world. They display a unique sense of purpose, principle, and permanence because they are mostly untainted by politics or by the fashion of the day. They are the engines of innovation that drives American economy.

Resiliency. As citizens of a frontier nation, Americans are a resilient people in their personal lives as well as their social, economic, and political systems. Flexibility and self-reliance are other important aspects of the American culture. In the last ten years, the US economy faced and overcame a number of major challenges—the collapse of the technology-driven stock market, corporate scandals like Enron and Lehman Brothers, the World Trade Center attacks of September 11 in 2001, the Afghanistan and Iraq wars, and a disastrous hurricane along the Louisiana coast in 2005. But none of these broke the American spirit. Americans picked up the pieces and moved on.

155

Pop culture. American culture has been internationalized in many ways especially by the younger generation. It exhibits incredible creativity in classical, modern, and postmodern arts, music, science, and technology. Further, this participation in creation and enjoyment is widespread. It is not confined to the high-brow society. There is no class distinction here. American pop culture is for everybody and is a major popular export item around the world.

Immigration. America is a multicultural rainbow of hope and opportunity. It has been and still is a magnate and a desired destination for people from all over the world. They come here to follow their hopes and dreams and beliefs without fear of repression or discrimination. This is a land of immigrants, and there is no place on earth that is better at welcoming with open arms immigrants who want to be a part of Americana, respect and obey its laws, and become responsible and contributing members of the society. Americans have a remarkable *"love thy neighbor"* attitude. One of the most spectacular and gratifying sights in the world is the peaceful, happy, and colorful pageantry of comingling humanity of all races and nationalities from around the globe in a truly cosmopolitan place like the Times Square in New York. You see there, at all times, people of all colors—white, black, yellow, and brown; young and old; men and women; people of all professions and beliefs, Christians, Moslems, Jews, and Hindus—doing their thing, living, and letting live. The only thing that matters is that they are members of the human race, brothers and sisters. This can happen only in America.

Diversity. No nation is as sensitive to and understanding of diversity in people's cultures and religions as is the US. The old concept of America the "melting pot" has been replaced by a new more palatable and equitable idea of a "flower pot," meaning no group has to lose its distinctive characteristics to become American. Each group can retain its identity and still, together, they all create a vibrant nation with an unmatched cultural diversity. Americans recognize and appreciate the value of diversity in evolving and enriching their unique national culture.

Charity. Americans are among the most charitable people in the world. Be it international disasters like the tsunami of 2004 or a simple local mishap, Americans are the first to reach out with a helping hand.

Can-do spirit. America is at its very best in collective problem solving with extraordinary organization, discipline, and imagination. There are innumerable examples of this at the national and local levels but none better than the rescue of the crippled Apollo 13 spacecraft or the lost miners in underground coal mines or the rescue of eighteen-month-old Jessica McClure who fell and was trapped twenty-two-feet below ground in an abandoned well (a mere eight-inches in diameter) in the backyard of the family home in West Texas. Jessica's amazing rescue took some fifty-eight hours and used the then relatively new technology of water jet cutting. The way the entire nation prays, comes together, supports, and executes such high-risk challenges is the ultimate testimony to the quintessential American spirit.

True democracy. Compared to most other countries, the common man's life in America is clean, free of corruption, and based on the principles of democracy. Political and social systems and procedures are generally well-established, and things work here as they are supposed to.

America never had royalty, and as a result, there is no hierarchical culture. This is a fundamental reason for the essential sense of equality of opportunity among all citizens. Societies that have evolved from hierarchical structures, even though they may be democratic today, are prone to social inequality. They tend to retain undercurrents of privilege that invariably lead to favor seeking, dependence of one group on another, possible exploitation, and opportunity for corruption by the people in power. This is evident in countries like India. Ingrained in the mass thinking in such places is the sense of dependence on some deity, some rajah, or some omnipotent politician for all their needs. There is little sense of participation in the democratic process. This lack of intelligent and active involvement opens the doors for unscrupulous politicians to begin to behave as if they are kings and gods and exploit the masses.

THE PROBLEM

The foregoing paragraphs describe some of the values that have made America great. In a very fundamental sense, the American people are hardworking, decent, and fair. America has been a world leader for over a century in almost all spheres of human activity, in providing opportunity and creating wealth. However, today the shift in the national environment and attitudes is unmistakable as described earlier in this essay.

It is hard to attain the number 1 position, but it is harder to retain it. America is in real danger of losing its edge unless specific, concrete steps are taken to regain its leadership in the world and restore the quality of life for its people. But with determination and vision, it is all achievable.

America is the envy of the world in many ways. Americans are lucky to have been born here. Immigrants are thankful to have been admitted to this land where the government does protect the citizens and their liberties, where the rule of law is supreme, and where private property is safe.

However, somewhere along the path, exaggerated self-interest has taken Americans off the track. America needs to reinstate its basic values—equality of human beings, responsibility to help one another, and commitment to liberty for all people. America needs to be responsive and ensure that the system meets the changing needs of all citizens in the face of the changing global environment.

SOME IDEAS

Politicians, sociologists, educationists, industry and community leaders, churches, and families all need to assess what is happening in their sphere of influence, evaluate where they are going, and refocus on their values and goals. At the very minimum, some of the obvious things to address are as follows:

1. Revamp elementary and high school education emphasizing math, science, independent thinking, and team work.
2. Emphasize and support education at all levels. Ensure that interest rates on educational loans are the lowest—certainly lower than those on real estate, automobiles, appliances, etc.
3. Conduct comprehensive tax reform retaining its progressive nature. The current tax code is too complex with too many loop holes.
4. To alleviate unemployment, institute a thirty-six—to thirty-eight-hour work week, three-week minimum vacation and mandatory retirement age around sixty-two to sixty-five. This will solve the unemployment problem, and in general, people will be more relaxed and happier.
5. Tax disposable paper and plastic products heavily to discourage waste. Increase taxes on newsprint. Eliminate bulk rate for mail.
6. Close certain businesses, especially shopping malls, at least one day a week and restrict shopping hours. (Reinstate the "blue law.")
7. Increase gasoline tax and promote public transportation where possible. The current US energy consumption patterns are not sustainable in

the long run. Alternative fuels will help but are not the solution. What is needed is a meaningful reduction in consumption.

8. Demand higher energy efficiency standards on cars and housing construction. Heating and cooling of large, improperly insulated homes is a major drain on energy.

9. Revamp the Primary Election system. The current process is too long, divisive, and unnecessarily expensive.

10. Establish term limits for all elected offices. People get comfortable and stagnant in their jobs after a certain period. The nation needs a constant renewal through new blood and new ideas.

11. Establish and enforce strict gun control laws. The United States is the only country in the civilized world without adequate gun control. At the very minimum, there should be strict licensing requirements.

12. Forget "nation building" in other lands. Do it at home. Support the United Nations, fully empowering it for what it was intended to do. The US is a generous and charitable nation. But it does not need to police the world or try to solve all of its problems.

13. Recognize that America is not always going to be the leader in everything it does. Keep an open mind and learn from others. Evaluate how VAT, universal health care, gun control, public transportation work, and how real equality for women is achieved in some of the European countries. Adopt their best practices where possible.

14. America's economic problems are at least partly due to globalization that was supposed to have been an advantage of opening up large markets in the developing world. However, most of the developed countries completely missed in their calculations the impact of the billions of low-wage workers from the poorer countries entering the global labor market.

In the light of this, America needs a new paradigm to balance globalization with its brand of free enterprise, capitalism, and democracy. It should be ready for a greater involvement of the state in the creation of jobs and enhanced competitiveness through better infrastructure development. After all, globalization should not be a zero-sum game. India and China cannot continue to grow at the expense of others. Innovative, game-changing ideas have large global markets; and more often than not, such ideas have come from the US through great companies like Intel, Microsoft, Twitter, Facebook, Apple, and Google to name just a few. America needs to do everything to ensure that this continues.

In summary, America is at crossroads. While it is on solid constitutional foundations, its socioeconomic fabric may be fraying. But Americans are fair, hardworking and innovative people. America can realize its full potential by a serious midcourse correction for restoring its basic values.

(An earlier version of this article was serialized in Indo-American News*)*

FIFTEEN

American Universities

GRADUATION—A RITE OF PASSAGE

College education and graduation are among the most wonderful aspects of American life. Education is the key to a nation's future. America is blessed with some of the finest universities in the world. Graduation from college is a rite of passage. Commencement ceremonies at American universities have become the most joyous occasions of family gatherings and parental pride. Graduations are important transitions for the individuals, but perhaps even more so for the parents who no longer have just a child but an equal in every sense of the word. Graduations are a renewal of life. They represent a beginning with new horizons for the child; the completion of a cycle of life for the parent and a valuable asset for the nation's growth and well-being.

I n his highly acclaimed poem "The Psalm of Life," Longfellow says *"Life is real, life is earnest."* Nowhere is it truer than in the magnificent commencement ceremonies at universities across the nation. Despite all the talk about the decline of American leadership today, American universities, unparalleled in resources and quality, are an invaluable asset and envy of the world. They display a unique sense of purpose, principle, and permanence not seen in any other form of human endeavor. Commencements are periodic celebrations of the achievements of the students as well as the universities.

What is born must die. The old must make way for the new. This is an eternal law of the universe. All things in nature are cyclic with a well-defined life span. They rejuvenate, are revitalized, are born again. In the human life cycle, birth, puberty, marriage, and death mark significant transitions.

In modern societies in which livelihoods and careers are knowledge-based, as it is happening more and more so in America today, graduation from college must rank among these major transitions as a great rite of passage. It is a milestone where children, already physical adults, become responsible individuals equipped with the education and tools of modern trade ready to take on the world. Boys become men. Girls become women. According to the Hindu philosophy, this is a point of marking the completion of the first quarter of human life, *Bramhacharyashram*, and the beginning of the next phase, *Grihasthashram*—in which, having completed the education earlier, one is ready to raise a family, be productive, and contribute to the society in a responsible way.

REFLECTIONS ON GRADUATION

Parents of graduating college students are middle-aged by definition. At that age, in a majority of cases, your career has reached a plateau. You are beginning to slow down, frequently with unfinished dreams and uncomfortable, grudging realizations that you have gone just about as far as talent or fortune will take you. Right at that point of self-doubt emerges a confidence booster. It comes in the form of the bright-eyed, healthy, energetic child of your own blood and flesh, a revised, improved, and bolder version of you—so full of hope and ambition, new ideas, and new education, ready to take on the world. There is a chance after all, you think. Life begins again. Your unfinished dreams might yet be accomplished. The feeling of this vicarious joy has no parallel.

I experienced this blissful state of mind recently when our daughter graduated from law school. It is hard to believe that the little angel (only sometimes a little bratty) that just a few years ago you chauffeured around from soccer to piano to tennis lessons is now an attorney or a physician or a scientist as the case may be. Children grow up way too fast, and certainly faster than you think. As life unfolds itself in its many splendors, one of its supreme joys is to see your child successfully launched in this highly competitive, beautiful, but sometimes treacherous world.

COMMENCEMENT CEREMONIES

Typical commencement ceremonies at American universities have attained an impressive standard of excellence and my daughter's was no exception with its colorful pageantry of the academic procession and the overall elegant and festive ambience. The entire program, from the beginning invocation to the conclusion, was beautifully orchestrated with precise timing and protocols, inspiring and articulate speeches with beautiful organ music in between.

It is truly uplifting to see the next generation, our future leaders, so well-dressed, handsome and assured, poised to embark on a new life, not only for themselves but for their parents, their communities, and indeed, the whole nation. All you see is pure joy over a well-accomplished task oozing out of the radiant faces of the proud parents around you as each degree recipient's name is announced or the name lights up on a large electronic screen.

A RITE OF PASSAGE

Graduations are true rites of passage. They are important transitions for the individuals, but perhaps even more so for the parents who no longer have just a child but an equal in every sense of the word. Graduations are a renewal of life. They are a new beginning with new horizons for the child, the completion of a cycle of life for the parent. Your dream is their future. Graduations are solemn but exciting, serious but joyful all at the same time. They are great for family reunion and bonding, reflection and planning, celebrating and being thankful. Our graduations and commencement ceremonies are wonderful traditions that should never change.

THE ROLE AND VALUE OF UNIVERSITIES

Apart from the sense of achievement, pride and personal gratification that come from college education, and a potentially prosperous future at the personal level, its real benefits accrue to the society at large. The difference between successful and unsuccessful nations is the level and quality of education of their citizenry.

The duke of Wellington is said to have remarked that "the victory at Waterloo was won on the playing fields of Eton." This profound concept is truer today than it was at Wellington's time. It stands to reason that the contest for global leadership in this century will be won on the campuses of the world's universities. In this contest, the US has a great advantage. A recent ranking of global universities lists thirty-six American universities among the top fifty in the world, with eight of the top ten in the US.

Naturally, the US is the premiere destination for international students. Further, higher education systems around the world seek to emulate the key strengths of American universities that provide a model for best practices. One of the important features of American universities is the vast number of academic options available for study. The US is a large country with enormous resources, and almost every possible field of study is available in its universities.

The extent and quality of research carried out in American universities are impressive in their range and depth. Complete academic freedom, multidisciplinary approach that encompasses the whole gamut of basic and applied sciences, technology and engineering, social sciences, arts, and humanities are the hallmarks of American universities. That advantage coupled with the customary partnerships with federal government and industry makes the universities financially stronger and more effective in their impact.

In reality, universities do a lot more than the education they provide. In his excellent article entitled "Universities: Their Value to Society Extends Well beyond Research" Robert M. Berdahl, president, Association of American Universities, gives a comprehensive analysis of the real contribution of universities to societal well-being. He points out the following important benefits:

- Addressing urgent challenges with science
- Improving public policy through social sciences

- Enriching human experience through the humanities and the arts
- Enhancing civic and economic life
- Being champions of free society

Great American universities are engines of innovation, economic growth, and capital buildup. Research conducted by them leads to the creation of new technologies, new businesses, and new jobs that are needed to enable the nation's long-term economic competitiveness.

Further, universities are temples of critical thinking, reflection, and intellectual intercourse. Since the times of the Greek philosophers, the study of humanities has enlightened mankind as to the nature of truth and the concepts of good and bad, right and wrong—as the basic dimensions of understanding that give meaning, purpose, and grace to our existence.

A measure of the public good of American universities is in the intangible contributions they make through a population enlightened in the philosophic framework for a nation that strives to promote and support freedom throughout the world. It is a matter of great pride for parents of graduating students to know that their children can participate in this process and be responsible contributing members of the society.

SCANDINAVIA

The Scandinavia That I Saw

Of Capitalism and Socialism

To be a Woman in Sweden

The Heart Is Heavy

The City Hall, Stockholm
Home of the Nobel Prize ceremony

SIXTEEN

The Scandinavia That I Saw

The four Scandinavian countries—Denmark, Finland, Norway, and Sweden are similar in many ways. Their relatively small populations occupy large land masses of pristine natural beauty. Scandinavia is affluent, civilized, cultured, peaceful, safe, uncrowded, and environmentally and socially responsible. In global surveys on various measures such as quality of life, education, and business environment, these countries are almost always near the top. Their successful socioeconomic models have several elements that should be of interest to other countries.

For a great majority of people in countries like the United States, a two-week vacation in Europe is a much coveted once-in-a-lifetime experience. And here I am, based in Sweden and enjoying a vacation-like stay there for six months annually for the past several years. For a travel lover like me, this is a stroke of good fortune and an opportunity without parallel. With an easy access to essentially all of Europe, there is so much to see, so much to learn, and so much to experience. So many great cities in so many countries with their unique histories, cultures, and lifestyles, and all are within easy reach from almost any location in this region. Indeed, I do feel like the proverbial kid in the candy store who does not know where to start and what to grab. But no matter what he does, it is equally enjoyable.

A significant part of my stay in Europe has been in Vasteras, a typical small Swedish town located on Lake Malaren, some one hundred kilometers west of Stockholm. However, I have had the opportunity to visit a number of places in other parts of Scandinavia, large and small towns, using all available modes of transportation—cruise ships, boats, trains, buses, planes, and private cars. I have observed the everyday activities of the local people, and I have mingled with corporate executives at formal affairs. I have had a chance to visit some universities, follow the elections, and understand the social systems and some of their implications. This essay is a record of the first impressions of an interested traveler who has immensely enjoyed the natural beauty of the place, the hospitality of the local people and their simple, safe, equitable, and environmentally conscious lifestyle. Here is the Scandinavia that I saw.

THE SCANDINAVIAN COUNTRIES

The term *Scandinavia* comes from a movement of unification that originated in the region of Scania. This movement was at its height in the mid-nineteenth century and was centered around the idea of Scandinavia as a unified region or a single nation based on the common linguistic, political, and cultural heritage of the three Nordic countries—Denmark, Norway, and Sweden. (These three countries are referred to as "three brothers" in the national anthem of Norway.) However, the actual political unification never took place. Because of their common heritage, Denmark, Norway, and Sweden are similar in many respects. Finland, also a Nordic country, was occupied by Sweden for a long time and is thus loosely considered a part of Scandinavia.

The four countries have more or less the same ethnic stock, and over a period of the past thousand years, they have fought with, conquered, subjugated, allied, or merged with and separated from each other at various times. Except for Denmark (although it owns Greenland), which is to the south closer to central Europe, the Scandinavian countries have similar latitudes (comparable to Alaska) and proximity to the north pole, similar weather patterns, similar flora and fauna, and in general, similar lifestyles. They have beautiful summers that are much awaited, loved, and avidly enjoyed by the general population; and they have bitter winters marked by months of frigid, dark days with no sunshine at all.

Geographically, these are huge countries with great expanses of pristine forests, thousands of inland lakes, large shorelines, and numerous islands. These countries have small populations and exceedingly low population densities. The populations of Denmark, Norway, and Finland are in the range of four to five million each, about the size of the greater Houston area. Sweden is the largest with population around nine million, less than that of New York City. What is further interesting is that in each country, almost 30 to 40 percent of its population is concentrated in and around the major capital cities located on their respective coasts—Stockholm, Copenhagen, Oslo, and Helsinki.

THE CITIES

Scandinavian cities look very similar with magnificent waterfronts and canals, architectural integrity, beautiful parks, excellent public transportation, and a plethora of monuments and museums. Of the major cities, Copenhagen is the largest, Stockholm the prettiest, but they are all very beautiful.

The standard of living is uniformly high. The smaller towns are replicas of larger cities, only not as big. Because of the ubiquity of water, almost all towns are situated on a large body of water like a river, lake, or ocean; and most people own either a boat and/or a second home on some waterfront. The water everywhere is pollution-free, natural blue, and people speak proudly of the phenomenal effort their government makes to keep it so.

Smaller towns mirroring the larger ones with an equivalent standard of living is the hallmark of truly developed societies. The currently fashionable hype about the BRIC countries—Brazil, Russia, India, and China—as the new economic superpowers seems ludicrous the moment one steps outside of their few showcase megacities into the countryside and smaller towns. In the recent past, I have had the opportunity to visit Rio de Janeiro and Sao Paulo in Brazil, St. Petersburg and Moscow in Russia, and Beijing and Shanghai in China—all of them wonderful metropolises in their own right, ultramodern tourist centers ever getting bigger and better and richer. However, they absolutely do not represent the rest of the respective countries where majority of their populations struggle for survival. The IT parks in specific reserved areas in countries like India may remind one of lush green oases but half the people in some of these developing countries continue to relieve themselves al fresco with no sanitation or sanity. While the state-owned research institutes in these places can detect parts per billion trace amounts of toxins in drinks like Coca-Cola and the local politicians can dictate a shutdown of the manufacturing facilities (as they did in India a few years ago) in a remarkably rare display of concern for public health and well-being, human corpses and animal carcasses continue to float freely in their rivers and lakes. Not so in Scandinavia.

SCANDINAVIAN LIFE

On such global background, the wonderful uniformity of affluence and the high standard of living in towns here, regardless of the size, is most striking. Scandinavian cities seem to be bipolar, having two distinct centers of hustle-bustle located not too far from each other. The first of these is invariably the central train station, the hub of activity and human interaction. These stations are a lot more than just transportation centers. Conveniently located, architecturally distinguished, fully equipped with shops, florists, and restaurants, they also serve as shopping centers and meeting places for teenage lovers as well as business executives and daily commuters. The second most prominent center of any town and usually within walking distance from the train station is the "city square," a very large cobblestone-paved area surrounded by the equivalent of the mayor's office or city hall, a major church and a hotel or two all housed in ornate historical buildings.

The city square is the home of an open market and almost always has plenty of flower beds, fountains, an occasional statue, sidewalk cafés, and lots of people. Numerous narrow cobblestone alleyways emanate from these squares leading to specialty boutiques and restaurants of all kinds. While American-style shopping malls and fast-food chains like McDonald's are aggressively invading much of the developing world, thankfully most of the activity in these towns still remains in and around these two centers.

A FEW OBSERVATIONS

Because the winters are long and the summers relatively short, during the four months of summer—June, July, August, and September—it seems that just about everybody is outside whenever possible and as long as possible. When you see so many people outdoors almost in a carnival environment, a few things become immediately obvious here.

First, it seems that the Scandinavians have perfected the technology of producing tall, slim blondes. Apparently, they must have standardized molds and procedures to ensure such uniform beauty.

Second, while you do see a few African and Asians especially in bigger cities, in general, the ethnic purity of the society here is quite striking. I suspect that the concept of political correctness need not pollute your thinking here nor do you have to attend hours of diversity training classes. There is not much diversity here.

Finally, in Scandinavia, in fact anywhere outside the US, you realize a big difference. Suddenly everybody seems so trim and fit. On the return trip, as soon as you leave other lands and reenter the US, everybody seems physically so large. And this is not just optics.

RESPECT FOR THE ENVIRONMENT

And then there are other things that are distinctly different here, the most noticeable and important among them being their genuine concern and respect for the environment. There is no better symbol of this than the ubiquitous bicycle. Relatively short distances, narrow streets, expensive gas, and even more expensive parking make this a no-brainer.

However, the local governments go out of their way to ensure a bike-friendly environment by providing special lanes, street signs and signals, and parking stands. The second most noticeable thing in this regard is the minimized usage of plastics and Styrofoam. Grocery stores do not automatically pack your goods in dozens of plastic or paper bags. You either buy them or bring your shopping bags with you and reuse them. In general, the average per capita garbage production here may be one-fourth or less than that in the US. Efficient daily street cleanup by motorized vehicles is a rather impressive sight to watch here.

WHERE ARE THE PEOPLE

The shortage of people is amply evident everywhere. But they cope with this in simple but innovative ways. For example, you pack your own groceries. Grocery carts are coin-operated. If you return your cart to the right place, you get your money back. In long distance trains, multitasking is evident when the ticket checker also keeps the coffee bar stocked and cleans up after the passengers. Clearly, Scandinavia needs people. There is need and there is room for more people. An aggressive, managed immigration policy may be an answer. America is a living monument to the successful immigration story. Increased immigration will fill an obvious need, add to the diversity, and further enrich the Scandinavian economy and overall quality of life.

The equality of women with men in opportunities and compensation in Scandinavia, and particularly in Sweden, is considered to be at the highest level in the world. Apparently, male chauvinists do not belong here for it is not at all unusual to see a woman driving a bus or a train while the husband pushes the baby stroller. About 80 percent of Swedish women work outside the home. Forty-five percent of the elected members and 50 percent of ministers in the Swedish parliament are women.

Things are expensive here, especially those that require human interaction, and a simple rule of thumb is that everything costs twice as much as it would in the US. Undoubtedly, Scandinavia means high taxes and high prices. But the people seem to be happy and certainly seem to talk and complain less about taxes than an average American does. This is so because the wages, productivity, sense of security, and the general quality of life are also high.

EUROPEAN UTOPIA

Scandinavia, certainly Sweden, has the image of a pristine northern European utopia. Indeed, it seems to have discovered a miraculous middle path that has allowed it to combine the best elements of socialism and capitalism to create a wealthy and socially responsible society. In this achievement, the government, business, industry, and the unions have acted in tandem.

People are happy because cooperation trumps competition here. Everybody is taken care of. The highest quality education is available and free, if you make the grade. Whatever the perceived flaws of socialized medicine may be in American eyes, it seems to work here and, in fact, makes people less hypochondriac. Subsidized public transportation is simply marvelous—convenient, modern, clean, and relatively inexpensive.

While the taxes are high, the returns to the community are commensurate. Childcare and maternity benefits are among the most enviable. Almost eighteen months of paid leave for maternity to be shared between father and mother (who may not be husband and wife) as they please is an invaluable incentive enough even for casual visitors to start negotiating with their spouses to have another baby!

With all the evident affluence, the gap between the rich and the poor is substantially smaller in Scandinavia than that in the so-called developing or even poor countries. In fact in those countries this gap seems to be ever increasing especially in the face of globalization and enhanced trade. This is certainly true in the BRIC countries that are much in the news these days, as the high growth areas and future world leaders. This wealth gap is due to one simple reason—the absence of established, time-tested, and proven laws, policies, systems, and procedures. Corruption is a business strategy there. These developing countries have much to learn from the Scandinavian economic model.

The economies of countries like Russia, India, and Brazil are controlled and dominated by a few mafia-like business houses. These powerful businesses are always ahead of the government and its legal system, operating in the gray area and amassing obscene amounts of wealth in relatively short periods of time. Such rapid development does not have the solid foundations necessary for a sustainable system. Progress is spotty in the BRIC countries and whether the majority of the populations there get to enjoy any enhanced standard of living is highly questionable.

That the Scandinavian model works is evident from the preeminence of these little countries in the various rankings developed and published by international organizations like the IMF, the World Bank, the World Economic Forum, Transparency International, and many others. Be it ethics in governance, education, health care, business environment, or the quality of life in general, the Scandinavian countries consistently wind up at or near the top. Just as an illustration, the recent findings of the World Economic Forum (WEF) on global competitiveness are listed in the tabulation that follows. Finland, Sweden, and Denmark are ranked in the top four.

Global Competitiveness Rankings

Country	Rank
Switzerland	1
Finland	**2**
Sweden	**3**
Denmark	**4**
Singapore	5
USA	6
Japan	7

These figures speak for themselves. Germany is number 8 and the Netherlands at number 9 is followed by the UK to round up the top ten. Norway, the fourth Scandinavian country is ranked at 12, just outside of the top ten but way ahead of Russia at number 62 and China at number 54. The WEF expresses a serious concern about Russia's institutions, China's extreme lack of intellectual property protection, and the fragility of the Brazilian economy.

Transparency International, a nongovernmental survey group has presented similar information from a different perspective. Its recent study finds that Indian, Chinese, and Russian companies pay bribes more often than companies in any other country. The survey found that companies in Switzerland, Sweden, Austria, Australia, and Canada bribed the least. Great Britain ranked sixth, Germany seventh, the US ninth, and Japan eleventh among the least corrupt countries.

The Scandinavians are peace-loving, non-confrontational people; and the work environment is cooperative, team-based, and definitely non-competitive. The governments officially take a peaceful stance in international affairs. I was stunned to learn that in Sweden, the sale of war toys is prohibited. This makes plenty of sense. As Emerson said, thoughts become actions, actions become habits, habits make character, and character defines destiny. One invariably wonders about young American children enamored with war toys like GI Joe figures, tanks, guns, and other weapons of destruction. And then you ponder over the Iraqi war, the Afghan war, and American military presence around the world.

The Scandinavian political systems and the election campaigns seem to be simple and straight-forward, focused primarily on local issues and on optimization of the benefits of the social programs. They have no illusions about liberating the world or bringing their brand of socialism to others and redrawing the map of the world. Vituperative campaigning and personal mudslinging are markedly absent. In contrast to other parts of the world, politics is pretty clean and low-key in Scandinavia.

SCANDINAVIAN PACIFISM

Scandinavian countries have been recognized as the leading pacifist nations of modern times. Coined by the French peace campaigner Émile Arnaud (1864—1921), the term *pacifism* means opposition to war and violence. It is not surprising that the first two secretaries general of the United Nations were from Scandinavia. The first was Norwegian Trygve Lie (1946-52) followed by Dag Hammarskjöld from Sweden.

Scandinavian countries have no death penalty; they are very generous in helping poor nations, have a uniformly high standard of education, no torture or abuse in their jails, and provide their citizens with the best welfare and medical care. These are the most liberal countries in the world about gay rights, abortion, and euthanasia—social issues that are highly contentious in the US and many other countries.

Scandinavians are descendants of the Vikings (dating back to the eighth century) who were seafarers, warriors, and traders. They raided, plundered, and colonized parts of Europe, Africa, and the Middle East. How did this progeny of a violent past come to be recognized as the most peace-loving, humane, and tolerant people in the world centuries down the road? Historians or sociologists have not been able to come up with a simple answer.

Here are a few possibilities. In principle, Scandinavians are Lutherans or Catholics but most are not churchgoers and do not practice their religion in the conventional way. As a matter of fact, the majority may be classified as atheists or agnostics, and there is no religious fanaticism of any kind. However, national policies are based on the concepts such as respect and justice for all, caring for the poor, and nonviolence. These principles are fundamental to most religions. Scandinavian countries have small, homogeneous populations and mostly adverse natural environment. The instinct of self-preservation can promote cooperation, teamwork, and nonviolence and thus explain the Scandinavian pacifism of modern times.

The Scandinavian countries remained neutral throughout the First World War. During the Second World War, the Germans attacked Norway and Denmark. Denmark surrendered quickly, but the Norwegians fought valiantly. Sweden was not invaded and remained nominally neutral during the war. After the war, Norway and Denmark became members of the North Atlantic Treaty Organization (NATO). But Sweden remains neutral and unattached.

PET PEEVES

Despite my affection for Scandinavia, I do have a few pet peeves. In fact, only one of them is a real problem, the rest being matters of personal choice and values. It seems that these people generally do not need to go to the bathroom outside of their homes very often for there is a remarkable shortage of public restrooms compared to the US. And where they exist, you almost always have to pay an equivalent of seventy-five cents to a dollar, frequently in exact coins, just to use a restroom. This must be the greatest irony of human civilization. Here, the education is free and health care is free, but just to answer a routine call of nature, you have to pay!

The no-smoking movement does not seem to have made it to Scandinavia yet. They seem to smoke a lot, and they seem to start younger. The percentage of cohabitation, divorce rate, and out-of-wedlock birthrate here are among the highest in the world; and gay marriages have been legal for over a decade. Just like in Alaska, the long and bleak winters see increase in both alcoholism and suicide rates especially among the elderly living alone. These are serious human problems, but the system tries to take care of all as much as it can.

So this is the Scandinavia that I saw—affluent, civilized, cultured, peaceful, safe, pristine, uncrowded, environmentally and socially responsible. It is hard not to fall in love with this place. One only hopes that its successful socioeconomic model, an ideal mix of the best of capitalism and socialism, will be scaled up and the appropriate elements of it will be adopted by other countries for their own good.

SEVENTEEN

Of Capitalism and Socialism

In recent years, politicians in America have maligned the word socialism by associating it with the evils of the Soviet Union. Socialism comes in many shades, and in its enlightened form, it can create thriving societies of happy people. Scandinavia, Germany, France, and UK provide ample evidence of this. While capitalist and socialist purists predict the deaths of socialism and capitalism respectively, in reality neither system can survive by itself for long. Successful nations use an optimum mix of the best elements of the two systems. A rational approach to policy making recognizes that weaker sections of the society need support, and the stronger sections need incentives to continue their innovations that lead to national progress.

I magine for a moment a typical wish list of ten simple things a hardworking human being in any developed country in the modern world would like. It would most likely contain the following:

1. Affordable, clean, convenient, reliable, and safe transportation
2. Excellent education system at all levels
3. Hassle-free, inexpensive medical care
4. Secure retirement at the end of a career of hard work
5. State policies and personal behavior respectful of the environment
6. Equality for women in all walks of life
7. Availability of outstanding wines
8. Manufacture and availability of excellent cars
9. Production of high-tech products and pharmaceuticals
10. A safe, gun-free, relaxed life with a high happiness index

This certainly sounds like the utopia that "Freedom and Liberty" chanting capitalists have been dreaming of and promising for decades. Alas! The harder the capitalists seem to run after this dream, the more it seems to elude them. But this list describes the reality of life today in much of Western Europe where it comes naturally, almost as a given, thanks to their much-maligned socialism.

In recent years, an insult for a politician or policy maker in the United States, where there is no dearth of profanities, is to be called a "socialist." Fortunately, this distortion is limited to ultraconservative right-wing talk-show hosts like the Hannitys, Limbaughs, and Palins, and to certain politicians wooing this group of extremists for endorsement and support.

TEN LIKELY ASPECTS OF AMERICAN LIFESTYLE

In comparison to the list above that describes the most likely life scenario in the socialistic countries of Western Europe like Sweden, Germany, UK, or France, look at the following reality of ten things that are likely in an average person's lifestyle in capitalistic America.

1. Personal transportation in own car
2. Questionable quality of public schools, expensive private education
3. High-cost health coverage—Medicare available after sixty-five
4. Insecure jobs and retirement, inadequate social security

5. Lackadaisical approach to environmental protection
6. Relatively low representation of women in politics and management
7. Relatively low-cost, abundant food supplies
8. Domestic cars cannot compete favorably with Japanese or European
9. Excellent high-tech products and pharmaceuticals
10. Freedom to own guns and a generally stressful life

It is an established fact that the in-country income disparities in the socialist nations from France to Finland and Sweden to Germany are substantially lower than those in an avowedly capitalistic country like the US. In general, Americans pay lower taxes and have bigger houses than the Europeans. The Americans are wealthier, but the Europeans are more relaxed and happier. Certainly, American capitalism has its advantages. But these lists do not indicate that people under European socialism are at any particular disadvantage compared to the Americans.

EUROPEAN SOCIALISM

European socialism, combining the best elements of capitalism and socialism, is based on altruistic and moralistic considerations. To a certain extent, it does involve redistribution of income and thus a reduction in the disparity of income and benefits. As the European experience shows, it is not the amount of taxes that people mind. It is the unfairness and waste in the system that people object to. If the taxes are used properly for the common good and if people get what they want, if their needs are satisfied, they are happy to pay their share of taxes.

Conventional wisdom tends to divorce socialism from market-driven economics. However, with an enlightened view and consideration of its overall total impact on the society, it is not hard to see the positive aspects of European socialism and its consistency with certain market considerations. Effectively administered socialism can favorably compete with capitalism as is amply demonstrated by the economic success and the enviable standard of living and quality of life attained by the Scandinavians.

SOCIAL BENEFITS

When income disparity is reduced, employees at all levels are happier; crime, of all kinds is reduced. When crime is reduced, there is a decrease in nonproductive social costs of jails, law enforcement, litigation, lost time, and rehabilitation. With guaranteed health care, the population is healthier, medical costs are lower, people are happier and more productive. Subsidized public transportation is green and less stressful. Free education at all levels means a highly educated and productive and, therefore, affluent workforce. Scandinavia has some of the best public-sector research universities in the world as well as innovative corporate giants in the private sector like ABB, Volvo, Bombardier, Ericsson, and Nokia just to name a few. If you add all this up, it is not hard to see that a socialistic approach can provide returns, at the aggregate national level, comparable to or better than those based on purely economic criteria.

DOES SOCIALISM WORK?

In August 2010, Newsweek published rankings of the best countries of the world based on a composite index of factors like health care, education, business environment, economic dynamism, quality of life, etc. It is not at all surprising that all four Scandinavian countries—Sweden, Norway, Denmark, and Finland—are in the top ten. For comparison, USA is at 11, China at 59, and India at 78. The Danes are considered to be the happiest people in the world. And despite almost eight months of bitter winter and heavy taxation, few Scandinavians want to emigrate. They love what they have. And certainly nobody is rushing to the US.

THE REALITY

Certain politicians given to fear-mongering have distorted the meanings of words like liberalism and socialism for their own purpose by confusing them with communism or Soviet-style monolithic state ownership and control. There is considerable academic literature on capitalism, socialism, and the comparison between American capitalism and European socialism. Partisan purists on both sides have repeatedly proclaimed the death of the other side whenever a crisis occurs. American capitalism was supposed to be dead as recently as the financial meltdown two years ago. Today with the debacle of the Greek economy, pundits are rushing to write the obituaries of the European Union and socialism. Needless to say, borrowing from Mark Twain, all these pronouncements of death are highly exaggerated.

Socialism comes in many hues. There is Soviet-style socialism, Scandinavian socialism, and the socialism in a large democratic developing country like India. In any case, the discussion of the comparison between capitalism and socialism is, at best, pointless. The reality is that no system can survive for long in its purest form. What most countries have is a mix of the two systems to meet their own specific needs. The US, the bastion of capitalism, is socialistic in many ways whether the politicians choose to acknowledge it or not. I do not know what one should call social security, Medicare, Medicaid, or the massive bailout of the banking system by the US government, if not socialism. Likewise, private enterprise thrives in most European countries classified as socialist and considered destined to be doomed by some.

Neither socialism nor capitalism per se is the problem. The real culprit is excess and mindless application of ideology or unrestrained greed, as the case may be. The Greeks overdid the distribution of benefits without corresponding increase in productivity. The American bankers misinterpreted free enterprise as a "free for all, loot as much as you can" opportunity. Both are failures of people, not of the systems.

Societies thrive on an optimum combination of capitalism and socialism. The weaker sections of a society need help and support. The stronger sections need incentives and rewards to continue their innovations and growth that lead to national progress and create employment. The issue of fairness is of paramount importance in striking this balance and that is always the contentious point in establishing tax policies. One thing for sure, all citizens of a nation have some social responsibility, and a progressive tax system is an essential component of it. Even the ultimate poster boys of the capitalist system, multibillionaires Bill Gates and Warren Buffett, support this position.

Call it what you will—socialism, liberalism, or European boondoggle. These are just labels. I will gladly take whatever it is, if it means drinking French wine, dining on Italian food, enjoying Swiss chocolates, riding beautiful trains, and trading the Chevy for a Beamer.

EIGHTEEN

To be a Woman in Sweden

Gender equality has attained new heights in Sweden. In the Swedish government and in the board rooms of state-owned companies, 50 percent of the positions are occupied by women. Swedish women are independent, career-minded, and enjoy total equality of opportunity. Due to visionary and thoughtful government policy, women have incomparable benefits during childbirth and subsequent child care. In this land of Ingrid Bergman and Anita Ekberg, besides being blonde and beautiful, Swedish women enjoy a life of rare equality and independence.

With its ninety-six thousand lakes and dense forests, rolling hills and snow-capped mountains, lush green archipelagos, and clear water streams, Sweden has a lot of natural beauty. But one of the most spectacular sights in Sweden frequently happens to be that of human beauty right inside Arlanda airport in Stockholm at the long SAS ticketing counter. Behind the counter, you see a line of Swedish beauties in their elegant dark-blue uniforms, all tall, slim, blonde, and blue-eyed, one undistinguishable from another. It is quite a sight. They say blondes have more fun. That may be true. But it seems to me that Swedish women have more fun for reasons far beyond their legendary blondness. It may very well be because how the Swedish society and particularly the Swedish government view women.

In any international rankings based on opportunities available to women or gender equality issues, Sweden routinely occupies the number 1 position. For many years now, men and women have equal representation in the Swedish parliament as well as in all government functional departments. However, what is most impressive is a counterintuitive fact. In all of Europe, the percentage of women working outside the home is highest in Sweden and so is the fertility rate at 1.7 children per woman. One would have thought the more the women in the work force, the lower would be the birth rate. Swedish women do not have to choose between a career and family. They can have both, thanks to Sweden's unique system of parental insurance and child care.

RANKING AND COMPARATIVE DATA

Various international agencies study issues pertaining to women's equality. Here are some of their findings. A United Nations measure, GEM, Gender Empowerment Measure, focuses on relative levels of women's political participation and decision-making power, economic independence, and earnings. The economic component is influenced by absolute levels of income. The data show Sweden to be in the top position. The US is in the eighteenth place. The organization Social Watch publishes another measure GEI, Gender Equity Index that relies entirely on relative measures, using a score of one hundred to indicate perfect equality. This measure also puts Scandinavian countries in the top category, with a score over eighty; the United States has a score of sixty-five. The World Economic Forum's Gender Gap Index, GGI, combines quantitative measures with some qualitative measures based on a survey of nine thousand business leaders in 104 countries. They also put Scandinavia at the top.

The most recent and comprehensive data are presented by *Newsweek* magazine in its report entitled "The 2011 Global Women's Progress Report" dated September 26, 2011. *Newsweek* examined the following five measures that affect women's lives:

1. Justice: Laws on domestic violence, marital rape, access to loans, etc.
2. Health: Maternal death, infant mortality, access to safe abortion, etc.
3. Education: Literacy, education levels, etc.
4. Economics: Labor force percentage, gender gap in pay, and opportunity, etc.
5. Politics: Share of women in government, senior positions, etc.

A weighted average score based on these five factors was assigned to each of the 165 countries examined. All four Scandinavian countries that have made gender equality an explicit goal and implemented policies such as universal child care and paid family leaves, etc., are in the top ten list presented below.

The Best Places to Be a Woman (*Newsweek* 2011)

Rank	Country	Score
1	Iceland	100
2	**Sweden**	**99.2**
3	Canada	96.6
4	**Denmark**	**95.3**
5	**Finland**	**92.8**
6	Switzerland	91.9
7	**Norway**	**91.3**
8	USA	89.8
9	Australia	88.2
10	Netherlands	87.7

SOME IMPORTANT FACTS

Sweden is one of the few countries in Europe that has a natural population increase, meaning the number of births is larger than the number of deaths. Sweden has the lowest infant mortality rate in the world and the second longest life expectancy. Most Swedish women have careers and enjoy access to sex education, contraceptives, and free abortion—a far cry from the situation in other developed countries. And yet the birth rate of 1.7 in Sweden is higher than in countries like Italy, Poland, and Spain where women are less likely to have careers. So Swedish women have careers, they are more independent, and they have more children. A visionary and bold government policy has much to do with this.

EMPLOYMENT

More than 80 percent of Swedish women are employed—mostly full-time, some part time. Karin Alfredsson of the Swedish Institute has done considerable research on women's issues. She says,

> The system is built on the idea that both men and women can independently support themselves. The tax system and national insurance regard both sexes as equals. Every person is taxed individually with no specific deductions for families. An unemployed woman receives unemployment benefits even if her husband is a millionaire!

Municipal day care centers take care of all preschoolers even if their parents are studying or unemployed. Sweden also has parental insurance that allows people to gain work experience before they have children and go back to work at the end of their parental leave.

ELDER CARE

In many countries around the world, the elderly are taken care of by their children, but the load falls mainly on the women of the family preventing them from working outside the home or at least restricting their working hours. Sweden differs from most other countries in its elder care legislation; adult children have no financial or caregiver responsibilities for their aging parents. The state and municipalities take care of it all—paying out pensions, making insurance provisions, and arranging care as necessary. Institutional care is excellent and thus very few seniors live with or even want to live with their adult children. Geriatric care is one of Sweden's biggest labor markets providing great employment opportunities for women. All this must suit Swedish women just fine—not to have to put up with your own mother-in-law and get paid for caring a little bit for somebody else's mother-in-law in the city-operated elder care facility.

SWEDISH HUSBANDS/FATHERS

Sweden is a place where it is not unusual to see the mother going to the office and the dad changing diapers at home. Compared to most other countries, Swedish fathers take on a great deal of the day-to-day care of their children. This also includes taking care of sick children at home while receiving benefits from the state. Sweden has a very high divorce rate; at least half of the marriages end in divorce. But divorced women can survive as independent women. Unmarried or divorced women receive child support from the state if the father is unable to pay. A common joke for Swedish men is, "You can change wives but children are yours for life."

Back in the seventies, the Swedish government realized that real equal opportunity for women could not exist if fathers did not take a more active role in their children's lives. In a visionary move, they introduced Parental Insurance, consisting of a state benefit—80 percent of the salary for an average wage earner—that could be split between the parents in any way they pleased for pre and postnatal care. Sweden introduced this wonderful concept of paternity leave to the world. Until then, there was only maternity leave. Here is how it works:

- Leave of absence in connection with child birth is provided for a total of 480 days. Sixty days are reserved for the father and sixty for the mother, the rest can be shared freely. For 390 days, the compensation is 80 percent of income, and for the remaining 90 days there is a fixed daily rate. Unemployed parents receive a flat rate.
- Parents may also stay home, with compensation for loss of earnings, to care for a sick child sixty days per year for each child.

Such thoughtful provisions of the law are a hallmark of a civilized society that cares for its citizens and is a boon especially to women who face the brunt of childbearing and raising responsibilities. These laws make it so much easier for the woman to work, have a career, and still raise a family.

GENDER MAINSTREAMING

Sweden has a gender-equal government and gender-equal parliament. But unlike other countries, this is not due to legislation or reserved quotas for women. This is the result of free choice of the electorate. Every legislative sphere incorporates the goals that are central to the concept of equal opportunity. This is known as gender mainstreaming. Since 1921, when voting rights were granted to women, Sweden has had a strong women's movement. In general, Swedish women are active; they don't just sit around and complain. They are involved. They have made equal opportunity a reality and a model for the rest of the world to follow.

The concept of gender mainstreaming is a powerful one; it ensures that gender equality is not a mere slogan or a forced one-of-a-kind special program. It is an automatic integral part of the national psyche. And it begins early at the kindergarten level where boys are taught and encouraged to do "girly things" like sew and play with the dolls and girls to play with cars and trucks. War toys are a no-no. The Swedish concept is that gender roles are obstacles to development, that children should grow into free-thinking individuals, to mature and to use all their talents irrespective of their genders. This is a revolutionary concept that will totally flabbergast parents in other countries like the US where the biggest joy of the parents is to produce and raise a macho six-foot eight-inch, two-hundred-and-seventy-pound linebacker that will destroy, decimate, maul, and kill the opposing football team instead of merely defeating it. Swedish parents and schools think their task is to raise human beings capable of critical, independent thinking.

WOMEN'S SHELTERS

Even in peace-loving Sweden, there are instances of domestic violence. The women's movement has established shelters to care for women in need; these shelters are well-organized and well-equipped. In a fundamental sense, Swedish women are eager to support women, get personally involved, establish organizations, receive government grants, and become part of the social system. The distrust of the state and local governments that may exist in other countries just does not exist in Sweden. Protecting women's integrity is a primary goal of the Swedish equal opportunity policy.

NO PROSTITUTION

While neighboring countries like Germany and the Netherlands have legalized prostitution, Sweden has boldly gone the other way. The Swedish policy on prostitution is based on the belief that prostitution is pure exploitation. It is never voluntary.

The Swedish law criminalizes the buyer of sex, not the prostitute. This law has had a powerful impact on cleaning up the streets and many other countries seem interested in enacting similar laws.

The Swedes are a very progressive and open-minded people. There is wide support for sex education for young people. Gay marriages have been legal for a couple of decades, and there is no opposition to abortion. Abortion may be performed until the eighteenth week of pregnancy upon request.

WHAT DOES IT MEAN TO BE A WOMAN IN SWEDEN?

What it means to be a woman in Sweden is quite clear. Very simply, it means not being a second-class citizen in any way shape or form as is the case in many countries around the world, including some of the most advanced. Swedish women enjoy equal opportunity with men in every aspect of life and can lead a dignified, respectful, and independent life whether they are single or married. And where biological differences must necessarily come into the picture, the state does everything it can to assist the women by leveling the field for men and women. In addition to being naturally attractive and all the real and perceived advantages that may come with it, it is clear that the largesse of the enlightened Swedish welfare state must make being a Swedish woman something very special.

NINETEEN

The Heart Is Heavy

NORWEGIAN TRAGEDY

In the summer of 2011, the world was shocked by the brutal massacre of innocent Norwegians by one of their own. The killer was upset by the government policy of opening doors for Islamic immigrants. A country of incomparable natural beauty, Norway has developed into an advanced society governed by a smoothly functioning socialistic system that cares for all citizens. It is heartening to know that the Norwegian government is going to stay its course on immigration. It will not change its policies of openness, tolerance, and diversity just because of this freak, one-time tragedy.

The heart is heavy and the mind is numb. It is hard to think and harder to express. The soul grieves for Norway, indeed for all of Scandinavia, where I spent a better part of the past six years of my life. It is as if a part of my heart has been lost. I have had the pleasure of getting to know these gentle people and enjoying their wonderful land, from the beautiful coastal cities of Oslo and Bergen, to the magnificent fjords of Ullenswang in the south to Narvik in the North. A luxury cruise in one of the fjords here is an incomparably divine experience unlike any other.

So I woke up in a state of utter shock like the rest of the civilized world on that fateful morning of July 22, 2011, to read about a bombing and shooting masscre that took seventy-seven innocent lives in peaceful Norway. Anders Behring Breivik, thirty-two, an anti-Muslim extremist set off a fertilizer bomb outside government headquarters in Oslo before his shooting spree at an island retreat where youth members of Norway's governing labor party were holding their annual summer camp. I see vividly in front of my eyes the picturesque island of Utoya and the historic building in Oslo, the places of this insane rampage.

Scandinavia (Norway, Sweden, Denmark, and Finland) today represents the most advanced form of democratic human civilization, the epitome of the ideals of liberté, egalité, and fraternité. But the Scandinavians do this in their own unique way with extraordinary appreciation for nature, sensitivity to the environment, and concern for the well-being of fellow citizens. To this end, the governments here play a significant role in public life to ensure a balance—a balance between a vibrant and innovative private sector and a public sector strong enough to do what the private sector cannot or does not do. It provides incentives for business success, and more importantly, security for those in need—the old, the poor, the unlucky—attaining a wonderful equilibrium between individualism and community responsibility.

American politicians, Republicans and Democrats alike, involved in the most unseemly wrangle for months during most of 2011 on the so-called Balanced Budget and Debt Reduction issues have much to learn from these small countries.

WELCOME IMMIGRANTS

Scandinavians are the most peace-loving people and wonderful global citizens. And now they are opening up to the world welcoming immigrants and refugees from impoverished Africa and the war-torn Middle East into a life of equality and modernity. It is a symbiotic relationship of mutual benefit. Scandinavia can use more people. The immigrants need work. And there is an element of charity and a sense of fulfilling the responsibility as members of the family of nations. It should be embarrassing to the US that these little countries with much smaller resources have accepted a lot more refugees from the Iraq war than it has, but it was the nation responsible for the war and creating the refugees in the first place.

So the killing rampage that the deranged local product, Breivik, carried out in the capital city of Oslo and the idyllic island of Utoya is most uncharacteristic of the Norwegian people. Breivik calls himself a military commander in the Norwegian Resistance Movement that is in a state of war to protect Europe from being taken over by Muslim immigrants. Even as an aberration, it is totally incomprehensible. It is an unfortunate fact of life that in the US, most people have become desensitized to such violence since it is so routine in American schools, malls and offices, indeed anywhere, but in peaceful, pristine Norway, no way!

THE VIKING PAST

The Scandinavian countries, and particularly Norway and Sweden, define pacifism. Interestingly, neither Norway nor any of the Scandinavian countries were such a paragon of peace even a hundred years ago. Descendants of the Vikings notorious as daring seafarers and ruthless pirates, the Scandinavians of the past were rugged individualists unconcerned with the rest of the world, living in remote lands untouched by people from unknown cultures, unknown places, and unknown religions like Islam. Scandinavia was ethnically mostly pure. Modernity was nonexistent. Communities managed their own affairs by themselves without outside intervention. Norway was unpolluted in many ways—ethnically, culturally, environmentally. People were self-reliant, totally self-contained with no use for governments or outsiders, leave alone foreigners. The outside world beyond their close-knit habitats meant total trouble.

THE INSANE LONER

There is no doubt that Anders Breivik's Islamophobia is an acute case of recidivism to the Viking era. His underdeveloped intellect just could not handle the workings of today's Norway that is a global supplier of energy,

197

that is attractive to migrants from other cultures and religions, and that is tolerant of immigrants from all parts of the world. Happily, this modern and open Norway is not the extremist Breivik's closed Norway. The rugged land that was the home of the Vikings has become the most decent, civilized, and increasingly diverse place that sponsors and awards the Nobel Peace Prize. Breivik is no representative of this land.

NORWAY TODAY

Norway has always had incomparable natural beauty with its fabulous fjords and snow-covered mountains and plateaus, some of them being the highest in the world. And now it has developed into an advanced society governed by a smoothly functioning socialistic system that cares for all its citizens. While the weather can be formidable here presenting its own challenges, the exemplary resolve of the Norwegian people is more than a match for it. The Norwegians are among the happiest people in some of the ruggedest environments in the world.

Thanks to government programs and national wealth generated by abundant energy resources, Norwegians have come to enjoy an affluence and quality of life for all their citizens that even places like the United States cannot offer. Today's Norway is a land of tolerant citizens where people from different backgrounds and different economic strata can coexist and grow together. The senseless, angry Breivik who hated the immigrants in general and the Muslims in particular, was a clear misfit.

THE BEAUTY OF SCANDINAVIAN SOCIALISM

Education and health care are free. And they are outstanding. Retirement benefits and women's rights are unmatched. Disease is rare, and poverty nonexistent. Things tend to work. Public transportation is fantastic. Roads are clean and safe. Businesses are honest and efficient. Public places, including toilets, are clean and odor-free. Systematic redistribution of wealth is an integral part of the governing philosophy. Redistribution is an awful word in the US, but it is understood and accepted here as a necessity for national well-being and not considered as an assault on personal freedom. The middle class is large and the gap between rich and not-so-rich is relatively small. The state provides unemployment compensation. Incomes are high but so are the taxes. And taxes are put to good use. People are happy.

The Scandinavians love to drink. But they are incredibly disciplined about it. For a dinner out, the group's designated driver can never be persuaded to imbibe even a drop of liquor. Alcohol can be sold only in government shops. Special licenses must be obtained for most endeavors because the state is involved in most. But the people love this. Nobody is jumping the ship. Despite all the economic belts and suspenders provided by the state, the Norwegians have not become too comfortable, lazy, or dependent; they have not lost their vitality and self-reliance. They have come a long way from their Viking past. It has been a dramatic turnaround from that relatively unsophisticated culture to be among the world's leading pacifists in a relatively short period of time.

It is heartening to know that the Norwegian government is going to stay course and not change its policies of openness, tolerance, and diversity just because of this freak one-time tragedy.

EPILOGUE

India, the United States, and Sweden represent three remarkable forms of democracies of our times. The United States is the oldest and most affluent, India is the largest and rising rapidly, and Sweden, representing Scandinavia, is among the smallest with its unique brand of a highly successful socioeconomic model. As democracies, these three disparate countries have certain similarities. However, each has its own problems, challenges, and opportunities. Here are some of the major themes discussed in this book.

Politically and geographically, India is one country, but in a socioeconomic sense, there are many Indias. It is a country of contrasts where obscene wealth and abysmal poverty coexist. India has made significant economic strides in certain areas but has a long way to go to be a developed nation. Its current culture includes high-tech enterprise, Bollywood, cricket, and special treatment for the so-called VIPs and celebrities in the fields of entertainment, business, and politics.

Indians are in a hurry to get ahead. Their public and private behaviors are different and inconsistent. The social culture ignores, accepts, and knowingly or unknowingly promotes corruption by breaking rules, ignoring authority, and taking shortcuts.

India's salvation will come from four distinct groups:

- Selfless patriots represented by the likes of Baba Ramdeo, Anna Hazare, and many others dedicated to reforms and educating and mobilizing the masses.
- Highly educated technocrats like Nandan Nilekani, Jayram Ramesh, Arwind Kejriwal, and others, products of the nation's esteemed

educational institutions like the IITs and IIMs, as they assume elected or appointed roles and bring honesty, sanity, reason, and logic to governance.

- The tech-savvy, go-getter, proud, ambitious, enterprising young people of India so many of whom are now flourishing all over the country in places like Bangalore and Hyderabad. This group is rapidly growing and with the world's largest number of people under twenty-five, the next Steve Jobs and Bill Gates are more likely to emerge from India than from any other country. India's youth will have a profound impact not only on India but on the world.
- The ethical, visionary industrialists, the good business people like the Tatas, the Premjis, and the Jains, just to mention a few; and there are many others that are making a big difference to the Indian economy by bringing in technology, providing employment, and creating wealth.

America has been the undisputed leader and a force for good in the world for over a century. However, it is at crossroads and is being challenged. In the last decade, it has faced severe problems—some self-inflicted, others out of its control—that seem to have shaken the will and self-confidence of the American people. It can still regain its position of leadership by returning to its basic values of fairness, hard work, and liberty and justice for all. America has the capability of bouncing back.

Americas is a land blessed with incredible natural resources, matched only by the equally incredible strengths in the American psyche. It has time-tested, streamlined political and social systems and procedures. The most notable strengths of America are its constitution, its great universities, and its diversity and immigration policy. The innovative approach, sense of charity, resiliency, and the proverbial can-do attitude of the American people are additional assets.

Scandinavia is characterized by ethnic homogeneity and uniformity of progress everywhere. The quality of life and the happiness of the people there is a vindication of the Scandinavian economic model. Scandinavia also demonstrates that the progress and well-being of a country are directly linked to the status and treatment of its women.

However, Scandinavia has a problem. It is aging with a declining population. To maintain the quality of life and even to continue to survive, it needs more people. For this, like it or not, it will have to depend upon immigration. Fortunately, there is ample land and scarcity of labor, so managed immigration is a viable and necessary policy option for Scandinavia. The United States is a great role model for welcoming and assimilating qualified immigrants as an important resource for growth.

The debate about capitalism and socialism is of academic interest at best. Capitalism is not flawless. Socialism is not all bad. No single system can survive for long in its purest form. Successful nations use a judicious combination taking the best elements of both systems. India, the US, and even small countries like Sweden have remarkable strengths of their own. With an open mind and a cooperative approach, they can learn from each other for the benefit of their respective populations.

INDEX

I

J

K

L

N

P